TATTOO

Secrets of a Strange Art

ALBERT PARRY

DOVER PUBLICATIONS, INC.
Mineola, New York

Bibliographical Note

This Dover edition, first published in 2006, is an unabridged republication of *Tattoo: Secrets of a Strange Art as Practised among the Natives of the United States,* originally published by Simon and Schuster, New York, 1933. For this edition, the three color plates have been somewhat reduced and moved to the covers, and the black-and-white plates have been backed up.

International Standard Book Number

ISBN-13: 978-0-486-44792-6
ISBN-10: 0-486-44792-8

Printed in Canada
44792808 2025
www.doverpublications.com

contents

contents

list of illustrations

Black and White Plates

FACING PAGE

list of illustrations

foreword

THIS book, though the first of its kind, does not pretend to be an exhaustive study of tattooing in America. I shall be satisfied if it is recognized as a pioneer study, opening the way for further volumes by other researchers. For one thing, the medical aspects of tattooing in America await their own authoritative and lengthy studies by qualified experts. Tattooing among the so-called criminals of America also deserves a treatise all to itself.

My book is not a strictly chronologic history of tattooing in this country. This history unfolds itself through the length of the book in rather irregular steps. I often retrace dates and entire periods or go ahead to more recent times when the nature of individual chapters demands it.

Tattooing of primitive races, or among the so-called civilized peoples other than American, is brought into the narrative insofar as it influenced American tattooing or was influenced by it, or contains some salient features of similarity. Cases cited in this book, when not otherwise stated, are American. Cases of British tattooing are cited rather frequently because of the natural proximity of motives and historical development to those of American tattooing.

foreword

The chapter on Faith and Magic, in a condensed version, has appeared as an article in the *American Mercury*, to whose editors I am indebted for their continued interest in my work. By-products of my research work on tattooing have appeared as two articles in the *Haldeman-Julius Quarterly* (now extinct) and the *New Yorker*, but of these I have used in this book no more than a few paragraphs, considerably rewritten. I appreciate the several talks on the subject of tattooing in America which I had with Mr. Lincoln Kirstein of the *Hound and Horn*, which helped to crystallize certain of the ideas underlying this book.

I wish to thank Dr. Walter Bromberg, Assistant Psychiatrist of Bellevue Hospital, New York, for permission to examine and quote his most valuable unpublished observations on the psychology of tattooing. Thanks are also due to Mr. Frederick C. Helbing, Superintendent of the House of Refuge on Randall's Island, New York, for his co-operation in my study of tattooing among the juvenile delinquents. I also appreciate the help of Mr. John J. O'Connell, Jr., of Bellaire, Long Island, and Mr. J. B. Johnson, of Williamsport, Pennsylvania, who gave me the use of their collections of clippings, notes and illustrations. Finally, an acknowledgment is due all the tattoo-masters in New York, Los Angeles, and other American cities who aided me with their interviews and their own collections of printed material and tattoo-designs.

I

women and love

1

WHY do people get tattooed? Very seldom are the tattooed aware of the true motives responsible for their visits to the tattooers. Some say: "So that they'll know me if I'm killed or struck unconscious." Others refer the impulse to imitation of their friends; or because they wish a memento of some event; or because they wish "to look swell." Many claim that they get tattooed "just to kill time." These reasons are evident rationalizations. The true motives lie deeper.

Professor Lombroso wrote that people of the modern age and civilized countries tattoo themselves in an atavistic reversion to their primitive criminal type. But only a small portion of the tattooed today are criminals or even semi-criminals. And primitiveness does not necessarily involve crime. With these qualifications we may accept Lombroso's theory of atavism as an important point.

The atavistic dream may or may not be to kill or rape or steal. It may also be to frighten off an attacking enemy, to win a willing woman, to invoke magic for legitimate and honorable purposes. The primitive desire for an exaggerated exterior—for tattooing, among other things—is, thus, not necessarily a criminal desire. But atavism *is* here, in tattooing. Man's dreams are his leaps back to the primitive, to his childhood, to his past of untold ages. Tattooing is mostly the recording of dreams, whether or not the tattooed are consciously aware of it. The American Indians knew this. They often said to the pale-face that much of their own tattooing was a memorial to their dreams. The American sailors, tattoo-addicts that they have been for decades, are fond of talking about their dreams. Witness any morning's talk in the foc'sle, or such an overwhelmingly popular sea-chanty as

I dreamt a dream the other night,
Low-laands! Hoo-ray, my John! . . .

. . . I dreamt I saw my own true love,
Low-laands! Hoo-ray, my John! . . .

Much of man's dreaming is, of course, of his true love—of his repressed sexual world fighting its way to the surface. Thus we should expect that tattooing, the recording of dreams, would be of decidedly sexual character.

The very process of tattooing is essentially sexual. There are the long, sharp needles. There is the liquid poured into the pricked skin. There are the two participants of the act, one active, the other passive. There is the curious marriage of pleasure and pain.

The sexual basis of tattooing can easily be traced through the preponderance of erotic (not to say obscene) designs among the American tattooed,—so many broken, bleeding, or united hearts; so many naked or semi-naked women; so many frankly anal designs on the buttocks.

With certain primitive tribes tattooing is a mark of puberty, love and mating; most of the tattooed are girls and women rather than boys and men. In tribes where men keep the privilege of tattooing to themselves, women express their protest and envy by calling men usurpers of this privilege. Thus in Samoa there is a legend that the custom was introduced there by the *goddesses* of tattooing. They swam to Samoa from Fiji, singing on the way their divine message: "Tattoo the women but not the men." With constant repetition the message became confused and twisted. When the goddesses finally arrived on the Samoan shore they found themselves singing just the reverse, and so, says the legend, the tattoo became the undeserved prerogative of the men and not the women.

The Ainu women in the North of Japan, as well as certain other tribeswomen, tattoo their chins and upper lips with an imitation of hair. Some psychologists explain this as an expression of the women's desire to attain the men's power; others say that this tattooed representation of hair is the signal of the young females that they have already achieved puberty and are available for mating.

There is a certain echo of these motives in the white man's countries of today, in England and America among others. It is a fact that many of those English and American girls who are tattoo-addicts get their first tattoo-designs at about the same time that they have their first sexual relations. Not infrequently a girl selects a design or a series of designs, but waits for her marriage and her husband's approval to order them onto her skin. Thus, as in some primitive tribes of the Orient or Africa, tattooing in the low Anglo-American strata is identical with the girl's puberty or marriage.

A significant court decision recognizing tattooing as, in effect, a voluntary sexual experience was pronounced in Boston a few years ago. Two young men were brought to court on a charge of raping a young girl of good family.

The prosecutor, hitherto indignant and energetic, suddenly veered about and refused to press the case, suggesting that the judge instruct the jury to vote the men not guilty. The change was brought about by a photograph produced by the defense, showing the girl with a butterfly tattooed on her leg. The prosecutor, the jury, and the judge decided that, though the two young men were hardly to be praised for their conduct, they could not be convicted, for the girl had been guilty of contributory negligence, having misled the men by her tattooed mark into taking her for a loose character. Though technically a virgin before the rape, the girl was, in effect, accused of being a person of previous sexual experience—because of her tattoo.

How closely, in some minds, the idea of tattooing is connected with the idea of mating is illustrated by the following letter, published in the London *Pall Mall Gazette* in the summer of 1894, and subsequently reprinted in a number of American newspapers:

> Dear Sir: I wish in all earnestness to make known a suggestion that would save many a broken heart among the sensitive and many a breach of promise case among the mercantile, and would considerably lighten the labors of the police courts and law courts. My suggestion is that every married man and every married woman should have a circle tattooed around the third finger of the left hand in place of or as well as a wedding ring. This would be a sign that could never be taken off or effaced and would therefore leave a lesser margin for the treacheries and tricks of bigamists and other great and small offenses against law, society and individuals.
>
> To make this proposition practical and distinctive, of course certain rules would have to be made. For instance, any unmarried man or woman tattooing their third finger to be heavily fined. Every widow and widower to add a distinguishing star to their ring. Every married man or

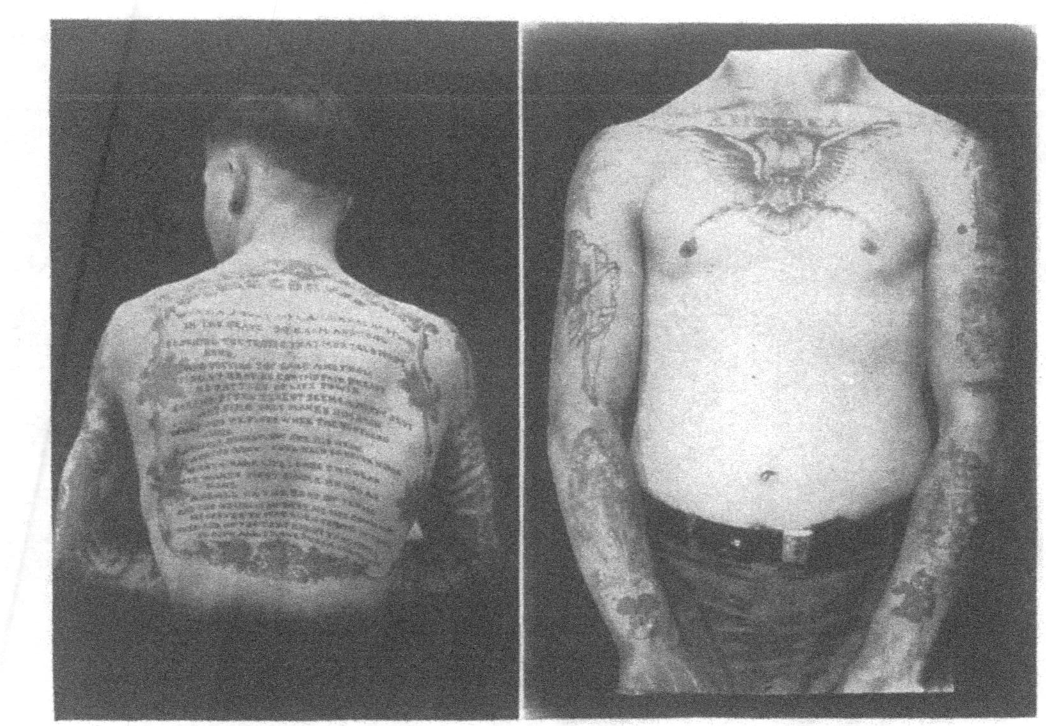

"What a jolly life a corpse must lead" is the first line of the cheerful poem tattooed on this gentleman's back. The front view is perhaps more affirmative in its sentiments.

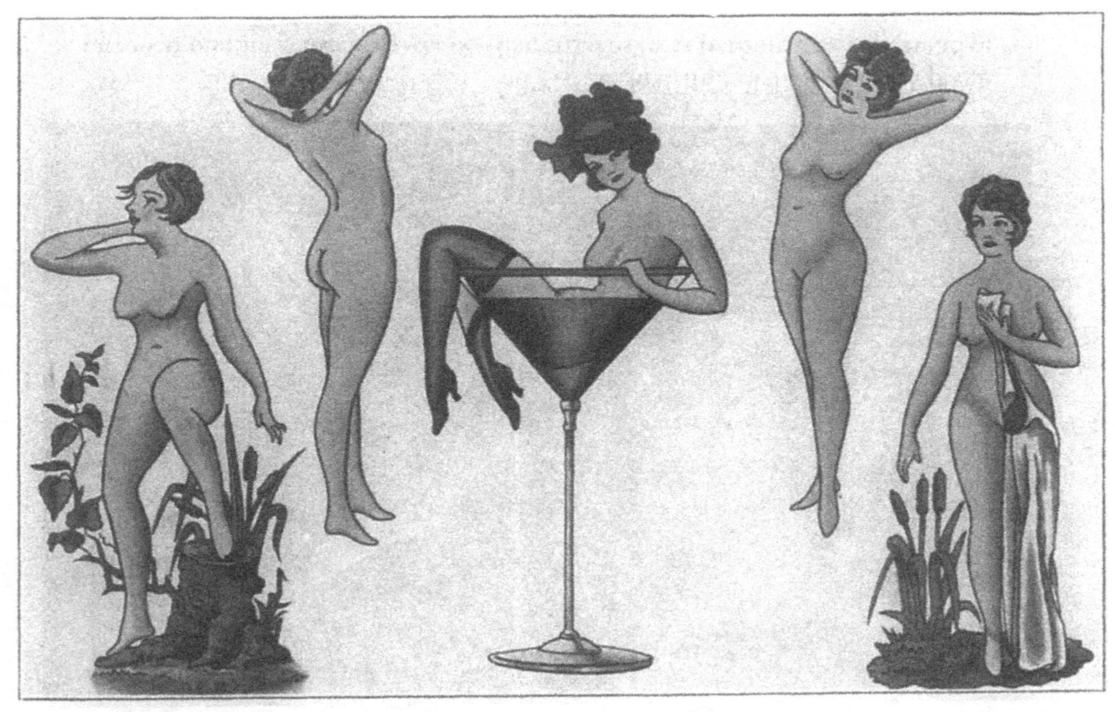

A few popular numbers. From the tattoo sample boards of Al Neville.

woman disunited by law to have a bar of erasure across their wedding ring, and those who marry two or three times to add the extra circles accordingly.

The operation of tattooing could, with all reverence, be performed by an expert in the vestry after the church service, or at the Register's office for those who only go through the civil ceremony. This tattooing may seem a return to barbarism, but our much-vaunted civilization has introduced such numerous aids to deceit that a safeguard and a warning, such as a tattooed wedding ring, would become a practical preventive of much sham, folly, and wrong.

Only those who have sympathy for unlawful liberty will demur against the idea being realized. I shall be pleased to hear from all who approve of my scheme and are willing to assist in forming a society to influence others in bringing about a custom that would help to insure peace, respect, and happiness to many homes and hearts.

Yours faithfully,
B. T. Knollys.

It is not known whether any tattoo-converts came to Mr. Knollys in sufficient numbers to found his society. But, in a way, he did find himself a successor in the person of the Reverend Francis Rawei.

A Methodist minister of Auckland, New Zealand, Mr. Rawei came to the United States some twenty-odd years ago. He delivered a talk before a meeting of the Cook County Teachers' Association on *From Cannibalism to Culture,* urging the husbands of Cook County to tattoo their wives. "I think this is a magnificent custom," said he, pointing to a large picture of a tattooed New Zealand woman. "These marks are put on the chin in order that the young men may know that a woman is married. When I go to Washington I am going to suggest this to President Taft as a convenient manner of conveying information of women's married state." Chicago, however, evidently would not depart from its notable conservatism.

2

The tattooers estimate, perhaps extravagantly, that today about five percent of all American women have one or more tattooed designs on their bodies, and that the percentage increases with every year, despite the bad economic conditions in which the tattoo-craft has found itself since 1929. Sailor Charlie, an itinerant tattooer, once gloomily assured me that if an American girl of the lower class gets stung by the tattoo-bug she becomes far more fanatic about it than any man. Eventually she will have much of her body ornamented in all the tints that a tattoo-artist knows, and she will change the themes, coming with surcharge orders time and again. But the connoisseurs agree that most American girls, those who are not of the sideshow ranks, are rather secretive about their traceries. Some of these connoisseurs have an extraordinary eye for tattooed girls and women. Thus J. B. Johnson, of Williamsport, Pennsylvania, a passionate collector of photographs and printed matter pertaining to tattooing, wrote to me last May:

> About two years ago I was in St. Louis and stopped at a soda fountain. I thought I saw a bit of tattoo as the waitress served me and her sleeve pulled back. Asked her if it was and explained my interest. Found that she was about 75% covered, about half of the work having been done by a brother. Request for photos developed that none had been made—but a short time later she went with me to a nearby photographer's where some good photos of her tattooing were made. I had to promise her that these photos will not be copied or published.

That evening she gave me a more detailed exhibition of her "art," and I must say that even now she wears as many designs as some of the platform folk of the circus and the dime-museum. The tattooing has been carried to the intimate parts of her body. She told me of two of her feminine friends who wore many pictures, yet no one outside their immediate circle knew of their hobby. This young woman made the very pertinent observation that the hardest thing about being tattooed was getting started —the fear of the needle pricks, and that old "bug-a-boo" that, somehow or other, a woman who has been tattooed is "not quite nice."

Not long ago, while on a train enroute to Norfolk, Va., I noticed, in the Pullman, an attractive, well dressed, middle aged woman, who had her name tattooed on her right arm, above the elbow. Later, chance brought us to the same table in the diner and opportunity for conversation. She had had her name inked in when she made several trips through the submarine zone, during the World War. Some time later she had gone to a tattooer to have this removed; instead her fancy was taken by some designs which she forthwith had engraved. This woman told me that she had about fifty different pictures on her epidermis, none of them appearing when she was in street attire.

Another diligent scout, John J. O'Connell, Jr., of Bellaire, Long Island, brought me a photograph of a young woman exposing her leg high above the knee with this tattoo: a heart with a scroll and the shortened, endearing version of her husband's name. She is a Brooklyn waitress, her husband is a professional ice-skater who works on ships between his contests and exhibitions. Of the lower middle class, they live in a brownstone house in a respectable neighborhood. She consented to have her tattoo photographed only on condition that it be reproduced in a scientific book, but never in a popular magazine. Like the women in the cases communicated by Johnson, this girl did not betray any exhibitionistic tendencies. Like her sexual life, of which her tattoo was a symbol, the design was something between her and her husband, not to be shown to the curious multitude.

The sense of guilt characteristically accompanying a sexual act is noticeably present in tattooing among white people, especially women. Tattooing is "not quite nice" because sex is "not quite nice." The American tattooers were puzzled and indignant when their high society customers ordered designs on parts of the body where they would be invisible to outsiders, or when they covered with bracelets and watches the wondrous snakes tattooed around their feminine wrists.

This guilty feeling, running simultaneously through sex and tattoo, has at least one perfect illustration in the American police records. Several years ago, in Newark, New Jersey, a Mrs. Florence Stichter disappeared, and scores of police combed the city and vicinity, spurred on by the anxiety of her husband. A few days later Mr. Stichter saw her on a street corner. She was half-hysterical. She said she had been kidnapped by a man she had known long ago, one Kenneth McDevitt. To her complete amazement she had been threatened and abused by the kidnapper. The husband, happy that she had turned up, took her back to Irvington, New Jersey. Here, in a moment of suburban intimacy, he saw on her left thigh a heart freshly tattooed on her white skin, with McDevitt's name in a half-circle about it. She said she was quite unable to account for it: when she awoke she found herself simultaneously with the eccentric McDevitt and the freshly applied design.

The husband called in the police. The police began anew. The results were somewhat startling: it was proved that Florence had lived with McDevitt long before she met

Stichter, that in the interval between these two gentlemen she had known a third man, one Charles Barr, and had been actually married to him, that she married Stichter without bothering to get a divorce from Barr.

She was promptly arrested and tried for bigamy; she wept bitterly. It is interesting to note that she denied her waking knowledge of both her intimacy with McDevitt and her being tattooed. She wished both to have been a dream; both experiences were equally sexual, and she had an equally guilty feeling about both.

There are extroverts as well as introverts among the tattooed women of America. There are, for instance, the tattooed women of the circus and the dime-museum, proud of their ornamented skin and making a profession of their exhibitionism. A feeling not of guilt but of superiority is their distinguishing trait. Carl Van Vechten pertinently observes of a Coney Island exhibit: "The Lady with the Last Supper tattooed on her back and Rock of Ages on her belly was obviously impatient with such women as were forced to wear mere clothes by way of decorating their bodies."* These professional women, plying their needles on the spectators, have done their share in causing the spread of skin-engravings among American females. Girls and women who would hesitate to get tattooed by men-masters not infrequently come up to the platforms of the Tattooed Ladies to acquire beauty marks or flaming hearts or pretty roses for their shoulders and arms. Literally scores of thousands of present-day American girls received their tattoo-ornaments in this manner. In the summer of 1925 alone, Trixie Richardson, herself an intricate exhibit, practised on the beaches of New Jersey and placed some 10,000 butterflies, forget-me-nots, and what-nots on her lady-customers. The post-War abbreviation of the bathing suit released the exhibitionism of many

* *The Blind Bow-Boy.*

men and women. They accentuated their semi-nudity by ordering tattooed designs upon the body. The American beach of today has become the favorite hunting-ground for tattoo-masters.

The main pseudo-reason advanced by the extrovert girls (of the non-sideshow type) is the improvement of their complexions. In the 1870's Martin Hildebrandt, a New York master, was afraid to tattoo the cheeks of two society women with a permanent red bloom.* But Dr. Marvin Shie, of the United States government service, states that as early as 1835, here as well as abroad, a mixture of cinnabar and red lead was used to bring "the natural color to the cheek in certain selected cases of superficial birth marks." After the birth marks were eliminated by surgery, the middle of the cheek was tattooed a delicate pink. Much of the mole-and-blush tattooing of today is ascribed by the tattooers to the World War experiences and experiments. Billy Donnelly used to say that his first case of permanent red cheeks occurred in the opening weeks of the War. The wife of a Canadian officer sent for him to tattoo the emblem of her husband's regiment on her shoulder. She liked the crimson which Donnelly was using on her and asked for some of it for her cheeks.

Later Donnelly explained that a white ink allegedly invented by a British chemist, when mixed with other colors, gave various complexions to the ladies' cheeks and had a permanent and non-injurious effect. Most of the American tattooers will tell you that they can supply a woman with a pair of eternal cherry lips, or, as Professor Jack Gavett, of San Diego, puts it, "fix a young lady with a nifty pair of cupid's lips that won't come off under any pressure." Charlie Wagner says that his first customer for a permanent complexion was a burlesque queen who explained that it would

* See Chapter VIII, pages 94-95.

save her a lot of time and trouble making up every day. However, a Milwaukee tattooist only last year cast some melancholy doubts on the complexion-creating business: "What we lack is the proper ink. It must be the correct shade of red; in fact, we must have several shades of red, so that a woman may choose her favorite tint. The red we now use in tattooing is too light and bright. We need one of a deeper shade. The proper ink may already be on the market, but no one has it in this part of the country." This gives one a glimpse of the technical problems constantly facing the profession. Nevertheless, even this pessimist agreed that the tattooing of eyebrows is a simple matter. The ladies who had plucked out theirs to keep up with the late eyebrowless era are entirely satisfied with the artificial ones inked in by the tattooers.

In 1927 Harry Lawson, a tattooer of Los Angeles, proudly displayed before me drafts of patent-applications, contracts, and diagrams, preparatory to the establishment of a chain of tattoo beauty parlors from Hollywood to Boston and Seattle to Miami. A group of plastic surgeons and beauty-parlor madames had entered into negotiations with him. The chain was to be a thoroughly refined affair. But the negotiations dragged on well into 1929, and 1929 proved fatal to this scheme as to many others.

3

The tattooers frown upon such innovations as the so-called sun-tattoos and paint-tattoos. They are not the bona fide article.

A summer ago sun-tattooing was reported as quite a fad with young girls at Far Rockaway, New York. The name of a boy-friend was usually "tattooed" by placing, on the girl's skin, strips of adhesive plaster in the shape of the letters desired, and letting the rays of the sun complete the job. A Hearst journal at the time of the fad rather sourly commented: "The new method is convenient for fickle lovers, as the tattooing is soon eliminated by taking a shade cure for a short time." Sensing a serious menace to his own craft, Charlie Wagner now mysteriously hints that he has begun negotiations with a certain manufacturer of chemicals. The manufacturer has a new pigment that can be needled into the skin in the old way but for a limited term, at the expiration of which the design will begin to fade and soon will disappear. Thus Professor Charlie hopes to save his needle craft and at the same time cater to the frailty of woman.

The paint innovation as confused with, or opposed to, tattooing, is really no innovation. There is a probability that Caesar, when he spoke about the tattooed Britons, meant that they were covered with war-paint. As early as the 1870's, American girls preferred their own war-paint to tattooing. On August 16, 1879, discussing the fad for tattooing among English girls, the New York *Times* recalled that a year or two before, "an Arkansas young lady, desirous of making a brilliant figure at a ball, called a paint brush and a quantity of red and white paint to her aid, and produced on those present at the ball the impression that she was wearing a beautiful and costly pair of striped stockings." The *Times* helpfully added: "What the Arkansas young lady did in a rough and temporary way, her British sister can do neatly and permanently, with the help of a skilful artist in tattooing." In our own days painted feminine legs are sporadically reported from Paris, Hollywood, and Greenwich Village.

On the whole tattoo-masters feel less incensed over the paint method than the sun technique, perhaps because the latter is usually mis-advertised as a real tattoo. Their indignation knew no bounds when a recent brand of lip-stick was widely publicized under the name TATTOO (". . . a surprising new lip-stick which you rub on, rub off . . . and only the color stays . . . true to its name, TATTOO, it *really* stays . . ."). And now, hearing of the ultra-latest fashion to decorate beach pajamas with the tattoo motifs of the American sailors, the tattooers do not know whether to frown or to be flattered.

They feel flattered because Miss Gwenyph Waugh and other creators of these riotous pajamas humbly descend from their Washington Square North studios to the Bowery tattoo-cubicles for the designs. They frown because, like the creators of the last summer's sun technique, Miss Waugh and her followers call their method tattoo when emphatically it is not tattoo. To be tattoo all these eagles and anchors and Columbias of the Bowery masters' sample-books should be on the ladies' skins and not on their pajamas. Nothing could be clearer than that.

From the foregoing we see how closely, with American women, the motifs of clothing and tattoo run together. Clothing with woman is more than a means of warmth or a concealment of the intimate parts of her body. With her, more than with man, it is decorative, a sexual adornment, a bait to the other sex. In this respect tattoo with her assumes certain of the bait-camouflage functions of clothing.* American girls, ordering permanent blushes on their cheeks, or perma-

* Among certain primitive people, the tattoo-ornaments were clearly thought of in terms of dress. In old Japan, for instance, rikshas, porters and other menial workers, who were compelled to work semi-nude because of the speed of their work in hot weather, felt their shame and inferiority and tried to substitute tattooing for clothing. The ornaments covered their bodies like beautiful dress yet neither impeded their movements nor increased their sweating. An echo of this clothing-element in tattoo-ornament is found in the so-called Scotch socks tattooed on the feet of some British and American tattoo-devotees. I also know of an American, the scion of a rich family, who has a bathing suit tattooed on his body; on closer inspection one sees that the bathing suit is made of a multitude of roses closely woven together. The area thus tattooed includes the sexual organs.

nent ruby-lips of the same tattoo-variety, or butterflies upon their shoulders, express their desire for beauty and ornament at the same time that they seek to camouflage the defects of their complexes and complexions. Tattoo, like clothing, relates itself to the artistic impulse but basically is born of sex.

II

men and love

1

THE late Frank Howard, an old-time tattooer and circus exhibit, used to say that tattoos to sailors, soldiers and miners were what my lady's ribbon had been to the knights of yore—a love token. Professor Jack, formerly of the South Street waterfront in New York, affirmed that in four cases out of five the real reason for tattooing among men is love fever. Woman is uppermost on man's epidermis as well as in his mind. With characteristic pertinacity she has managed to get on his skin as well as under it. One of the most popular tattoo-designs even to this day is Charles Dana Gibson's famous picture of a woman, "The Eternal Question," the hair swirled with devilish ingenuity into the curve of an interrogation mark.

It works both ways. If he loves her, he expresses the abundance of his heart in suitable designs. If he hates her, he still does. An American army officer had tattooed over his heart the name "Mary," with a lover's knot. Six months later he came to the same tattooer and asked him to add in bold letters: "Traitress." Variation: a young man had a heart tatooed on his skin, together with his lady-love's name. Two years later he returned to the Bowery shop to order a disconsolate footnote: "Deceived." A young man named Joe married a girl named Sadie and commemorated the event by ordering a tattoo on his shoulder blade: "Joe & Sadie." The romance cooled; the marriage was dissolved; Mollie supplanted Sadie. He came to his tattooer with an order to draw two lines through the inscription and to tattoo, underneath it, a new inscription: "Joe & Mollie." But the same fate soon overtook his new romance. Rachel now appeared upon the scene. The tattooer drew two degrading lines through the second inscription and pricked in underneath it: "Joe & Rachel." We have no records indicating how long this process continued.

In justice to women I must say that no such violent or subtly cruel outbursts are credited to them by the popular legends of tattoo-dom. Women are more philosophic, diplomatic, or sentimental. One young lady, prominent in Chicago and not unknown in New York, had a butterfly tattooed on her shoulder with the initials of her fiancé, "F. V.," underneath. Then she fell in love with another man whose initials conveniently were E. W. It was an easy matter to alter the tattooed F.V. to E.W. Mr. E.W., whom she eventually married, never suspected that he had had a predecessor even in this touching province of the initialed shoulder. He was spared the pangs of jealousy torturing those women who were to look at "Traitress" and "Deceived." It should be clear from these examples that not all the inflammatory or incriminating love letters are to be found wrapped in pink ribbon in the bureau drawer.

A man will celebrate his passion in a dainty design and then betray both his love and his tattoo. Take the recent Bronx case where a husband suing for divorce offered as conclusive evidence the chest of the accommodating co-respondent. The co-respondent, a swaggering British sailor, bared his chest before the jury and Justice Carewe, exposing a scarlet heart tattooed there in company with an inscription, "True Love," and the name of the woman in question. Justice Carewe threw the evidence out, ruling it insufficient. The sailor may have ordered the tattooing without the lady's knowledge; he may have been no more than her secret admirer. It would have been different had the sailor's name been found tattooed on the *woman's* skin. But no such evidence was offered, as generally the woman was far less cooperative in court than the sailor. Suit dismissed.

In tattoo, as in love, it is the woman who pays. The man does pretty much as he pleases. In America it is only comparatively recently and only in the navy that he is restricted in the choice of his subjects and has to think what the others around him may think or do about his amorous pictures.

The sailor, being a lusty man, or perhaps to disprove to himself and to others his frequent homosexuality, pictures his woman nude. Frankly obscene designs, in most ingenious variations, have been not infrequent on his skin. At one time so widespread had they become in the American navy that the authorities felt obliged to intervene. In 1909 a government circular stated, in connection with recruiting: "Indecent or obscene tattooing is cause for rejection, but the applicant should be given an opportunity to alter the design, in which event he may, if otherwise qualified, be accepted." Figures of naked women, even in the most spiritual postures, are included in this ruling. However, it is enough to tattoo a bathing suit on top of a September Morn for an applicant to be accepted. At the time one of the naval officials explained that a nude picture on a sailor's chest or arm was not really immoral but that it might contribute to his immorality or impair the morals of those around him. Said Lieutenant P. L. Wilson, of the Naval Recruiting Station in Baltimore: "There is nothing absolutely immoral about having such a picture on one's skin. The point is that it shows the recruit to be of possibly loose moral nature and the effect on the men with whom he is associated might not be a good one. We want clean-minded men in the United States Navy. We are a good deal like a boarding school, where the morals of the pupils must be safeguarded."

Less frequently it is the sailor's sweetheart or wife who insists on his morals. David W. Maurer, of the Ohio State University, wrote to me recently:

> Several years ago while with the Gloucester fishing fleet, I encountered a brawny Newfoundlander who, having been about somewhat, had collected a choice gallery of nudes, tattooed in strategic points all over his body. Since we frequently worked partially stripped, his collection was held in great esteem by our shipmates. However, he inadvertently married a pious lass from back home who, during nuptial explorations, discovered his gallery and promptly sent him off to the tattoo artist to have ruffled skirts and brassieres put on the ladies. You can well imagine the razzing he was subjected to when he returned to the fleet.

2

To the man, a tattoo on a woman or a picture of a nude woman tattooed on his own skin is a thing full of force, movement, life. Witness the popular American joke:

"I married a tattooed hula-hula girl."

"Why did you do that?"

"I wanted to see moving pictures at home."

There is the famed folksong about the Tattooed Lady whose pictorial points fairly throb with life.* There is the ditty, mailed by a tattoo-fan to a friend-tattooer:

* See Chapter VI on the Circus, page 68.

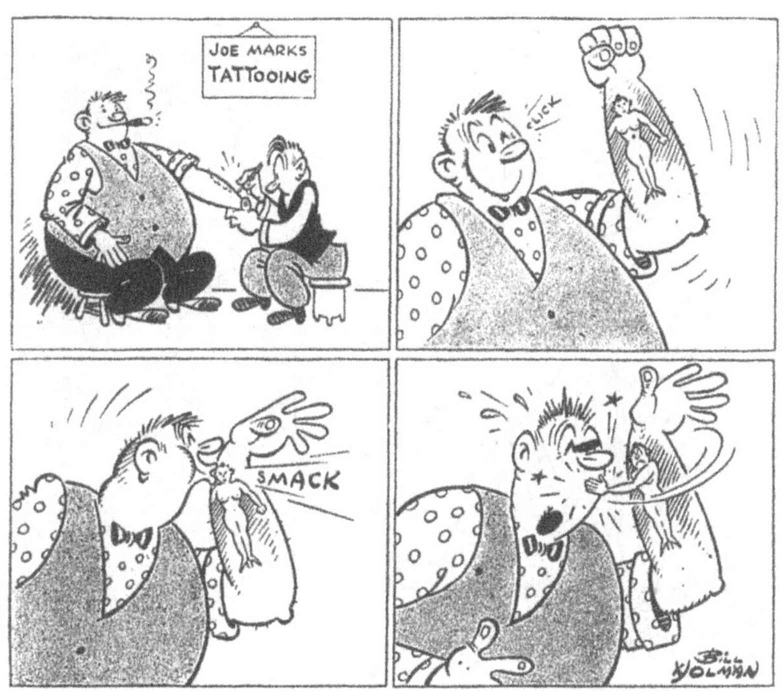

Reprinted by permission of *College Humor* and *Sense*.

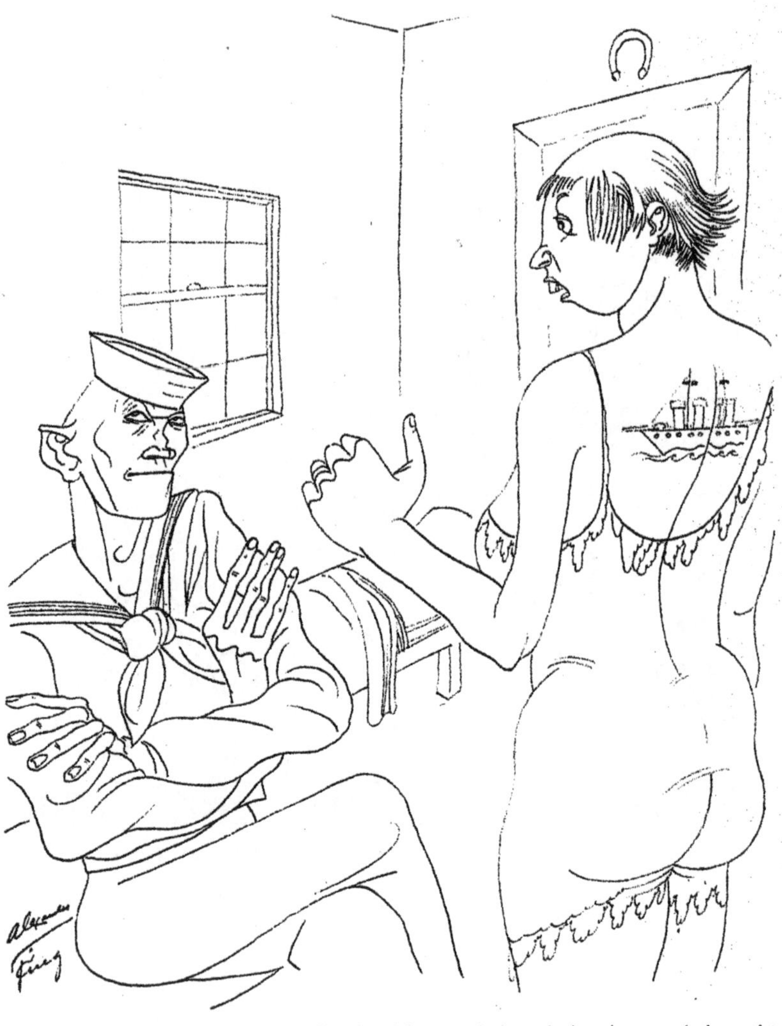

Reprinted by permission of *Americana* and the artist.

"Ya kin have yer divorce jest as soon as ya git yer lousy Alma Mater off'n me back."

men and love

A tattooed attraction
Is Dottie Drubbin;
Has a ship on her hip
And the deck needs scrubbing.

Again:

"I hear Mabel is reducing. Has she been successful?"

"I'd say she has. Remember the battleship tattooed on her back? Well, it's just a rowboat now."

There is also the story of a woman who had the Last Supper tattooed on her back. She grew fat with good feeding and now the apostles on her back are smiling. Another legend tells of a poor art student who was very thin. He had Leonardo da Vinci's Mona Lisa tattooed on him, for, even though he had his back perpetually turned to it, his reverence for the masterpiece was great and sincere. Years later, he gave up his art and became a brewer. Now he was prosperous and fat as behooves a brewer. His tattooer met him one day and wished to see his work of yore. The brewer obliged, and behold! Mona Lisa was also fat now, her sphinx-like smile had turned into the satisfied grin of a smug burgherwoman.

A few years ago there came to America a heavyweight boxer, Ricardo Bertozollo. At the time the newspapers ran captions under his photo: *"He has portrait of sweetie tattooed on chest. When opponent socks him on bosom, Ricardo gets so mad at insult, he flies at foe. That is, if he is able to get up."* The popular story about another boxer in America is that a nude woman, tattooed on his belly, smiles happily every time the boxer delivers a shrewd blow at his opponent.

Not infrequently when men order female nudes for their arms, they select masters who know the anatomy of the male biceps and puncture in the figure so that the proud possessor is able to make it dance.* Andy Sturtz of the Bowery says

* A similar process is sometimes followed in the tattooing of an American flag. The tendons of the forearm are wriggled, the flag waves. There is also

that among American sailors a favorite figure for these purposes is a hula-hula girl. A classic example of such a dance is cited by Jack Conroy in his *Life and Death of a Coal-Miner* (the *American Mercury*, August, 1932):

> Mike's arms were covered with tattooing. There were stars and anchors and serpents, but the most fascinating piece showed a naked woman. When there was nobody but boys and men about, Mike would move the muscles on his arms in a way to make the woman's hips wriggle. As accompaniment, he hummed an air he had picked up on the streets of Cairo at the World's Fair, and on occasion he would sing these words to the tune:
>
> *Oh, what a funny feelin'!*
> *Stepped on a banana peelin';*
> *Heels flew up and hit the ceilin'.*

The outstanding events around the man are accepted by him in close connection with a woman; he pictures, or looks for, a woman in every wood-pile. The World War was greeted by the male tattoo-fans with a rush for the tattooed representation of a Red Cross nurse accompanied by the inscription: "Rose of No Man's Land." The sensation of aviation is seen through the prism of girl-aviators, whose comely figures are tattooed on male arms and chests in countless copies. More popular even than Lindbergh are such flyers as Ruth Elder and Amelia Earhart. But the most common tattoo-design is any girl's figure, in an aviator's costume, with a robust inscription: "Flying High." Sometimes the name of the man's sweetheart is tattooed above or beside the figure. Some tattooists exhibit the patterns of such girl-flyers on the walls of their cubicles with terse come-on signs: "Popular Number." A girl's head in an aviator's helmet is also

---

a Japanese design, usually placed on the hip, showing a cat playing with a multi-colored towel. The design moves as its possessor walks.

known among the customers as the Queen of the Air. The tattooists say that the design is a special favorite with army men. But whether it is a flyer-girl, an angel-girl, a pirate-girl, a Red Cross girl, a geisha girl, a butterfly-girl, or any other girl, her features and curves are suspiciously like those of a hefty dancer from the burlesque: sensuous, coarse, *attainable*.

When a man neither loves nor hates a woman, but is merely afraid of her, again he expresses it in tattooing. Professor Jack Gavett says that a prominent San Diego resident had his wife's birth date placed on his arm "so he wouldn't forget it." Charlie Wagner tells me that his customers occasionally order tattoos of devils or human skulls or terrible-looking pirates to spite or frighten or awe their wives, "mostly after a quarrel." But this is just whistling in the dark. Wagner thinks that this method of counter-frightening a wife into reconciliation is, on the whole, more effective than the other method, of placating her into peace: namely, ordering her photo to be copied onto the man's arm, or having her name or their baby's picture tattooed onto the skin. Says Charlie: "They cry as I work on 'em. Gosh, you oughta see their tears. Not for the pain, y'understand, but because they're sorta sentimental. But it's no good. When the woman sees her picture on him, or the baby's picture, she knows she's got him for keeps alright, an' she don't care for him no more. You'se got to keep a woman guessing, mostly."

3

The sense of guilt is intensified in some by reason of the onanistic or homosexual character of tattooing. The sexual elements of sadism and masochism—the pleasurable infliction and endurance of pain—are more than evident in the act of man's tattooing. In 1881 a writer in the London *Saturday Review* remarked:

tattoo

> The origin of tattooing is, doubtless, the same as the origin of whittling—namely, pure brainless indolence. But while the civilized Yankee merely whittles at his chair, his table, or a piece of soft wood, the untutored and childish savage naturally preferred whittling at his fellow-creatures. He saw no fun in whittling at dead, unfeeling matter. The love of giving pain is one of the earliest instincts of our nature, and the practice is agreeable to the least developed savage as to the most accomplished modern libeler.

I see more than a mere coincidence in the fact that the old-time American sailors, the most womanless group of all, were as assiduous tattoo-devotees as they were expert whittlers and wood-carvers, practicing on ships' heads and all sorts of effigies which they carved and painted while on their long voyages. Even now sailors are tattooed not only in port, but (and to a greater extent than is generally supposed) at sea on their ships as well,—because there are no women at sea, and tattooing is a substitute. Rare is a large freighter or man-o'-war that does not boast an amateur tattooer among the crew. Billy Donnelly, a professional tattooer at one time operating on the Brooklyn waterfront, used to sail as such a seaman-tattooer on British war-transports. You will also find soldier-tattooers. Al Neville, now of the Bowery, used to tattoo his fellow-soldiers while serving in the British army.

The American frontier, a womanless phenomenon, has always been a grateful field for tattooers. The miners of California, the loggers of the Northwest, went in for this form of homosexual experience. Because woman was so infrequent on the American frontier, the awe and fear of her persisted in this country long after her rarity was no more. But now, even with women plentiful in all parts of the country, the sexual act here remains furtive and unnecessarily hurried, and various substitutes for it flourish. That is why tattooing has been so popular among the whites in America even within the last three or four decades when women have been abundantly distributed.

The sexual motif, whether or not conscious, also emerges from the cases of mutual tattooing among members of the same family, especially among the tattooed couples exhibiting themselves in American circuses and dime-museums. Jack Conway tattooed his wife, and she returned the compliment. "Red" Gibbons of San Antonio and St. Louis, tattooed his wife, putting so much conjugal affection into the job that for a long time Mrs. Gibbons was considered by connoisseurs one of the best examples of the tattoo-art ever shown in the Ringling circus. Frank Howard did some of the tattoo-designs on the body of his sister Annie. Professor Charlie Wagner, of the Bowery, tattooed the entire body of his brother Steve. The hint of incest was found to be so popular among the old-time American circus-crowds that many spielers proclaimed that the girl on the platform had been tattooed as a small child by her own father. J. B. Johnson of Williamsport, Pennsylvania writes me: "Not long ago I picked up a photo of a family group,—father, mother, daughter, and two sons,—all of the family having been decorated by the father, who learned to tattoo during two enlistments in the navy, and while he was being covered with pictures. All three of the youngsters, ranging from 16 to 22, are well covered with traceries. None of them is professional, i.e., they have not commercialized their decorations on the platform."

As for the narcissist-exhibitionist it may be said, briefly, that he has amorous designs on himself.*

* Further information about narcissism in tattooing will be found in Chapter IX.

III

prostitutes and perversion

1

PROSTITUTES in America, as elsewhere, get tattooed because of certain strong masochist-exhibitionistic drives. Feeling sorry for their sorry fate, they seek to give themselves more cause for self-pity by undergoing the pain of tattooing. They twist their inturning commiseration into bitter inscriptions full of cynical humor. Many of these may be easily imagined but practically none may be set down in these pages.

The story is told of a New Orleans woman of joy who had the picture of a hula-hula girl tattooed on the belly in such ingenious juxtaposition that by doing a semblance of *danse du ventre,* she gave her waterfront clients some highly entertaining exhibitions. Here we see a desire to hold or increase trade by unusual inscriptions or figures; as in the circus, the profit-motive is allied with the drive of exhibitionism.

Exhibitionism sometimes brings not only monetary profit but also physical protection. There must be something of this consideration, however inarticulate, when a prostitute orders upon her skin the name or even a likeness of her lover-protector or pimp. Thus, in the dock districts of the London

East End, English prostitutes have on their skin the tattooed portraits of their Negro lovers, much to the chagrin of the white American sailors. The old-time French prostitutes bore on the abdomen the names of their lesbian lovers. In America those frail ladies who specialize in marine love are noted as the most ardent tattoo-addicts. Acquisition of each transient sweetheart is celebrated by the affixing of his initials to the lady's arms or legs. Thus many present virtual walking alphabets and display wonderful mnemonics; they amaze even the callous tattooers by reciting the full names, ships and rank of the navy men standing bravely behind these initials.

However, the effect of such inscriptions and likenesses is often opposite to the one desired. They not only fail to protect the woman from over-rough handling on the part of men, but evoke male jealousy and wrath. But perhaps subconsciously this is the very aim of the woman: to be mistreated because of such tattooing, to suffer more and more, to have ever fresh grounds for self-pity. We note a clear masochistic drive in the old-time prostitutes of Algeria who, after quarrels with their lovers, would apply burning cigarettes to their arms or breasts to eliminate the tattooed names of their admirers.

Not infrequently prostitutes undergo tattooing on the most sensitive parts of the body, where the pain of the operation is excruciating. This is particularly marked among women of the East. Here magic-evoking and masochism become identical. By undergoing sacrificial pain the woman is calling forth the protection of the gods. In America cases have been noted of women of the streets placing the tattooed names and portraits of their lovers on the tenderest parts of their breasts. With such women, tattooing on the most sensitive and frankly sexual parts is in itself a sexual act. The sacrificial pain is also a sexual pleasure; the sacrifice is offered to ward off the lover's unfaithfulness.*

The very design often betrays an exhibitionist's striving toward pain: a tattoo picture favorite with American prostitutes of the lower category is a dagger inscribed "Death Before Dishonor." Frequently the dagger is tattooed in such a manner as to seem to be piercing the flesh of the woman. The same design, with the same inscription, is reported popular among male prostitutes, also among the more candid homosexuals in the merchant marine. Electric Elmer once said: "It is surprising how many 'Death-before-Dishonors' I put on. It shows the fine feelings and uprightness of the young men who come to me." The sentiment is a tribute either to Elmer's moral innocence or to his sense of irony.

2

In the 1890's Dr. Francisco Baca noted among Mexican criminals and soldiers tattooed pictures of the most frankly lubricious inspiration. Similar pictures may be observed now as then not only in Mexico but in the seaports and large inland centers of North America.

Such pictures in many cases may be explained by the men's heightened heterosexuality. However, in certain other cases the suspicion is that the men who order such tattoos are homosexuals who deny their perversion by insisting, often with blatant obscenity, upon their normality. The attempt is as pathetic as the desire of female and male prostitutes to prove their respectability with the "Death-before-Dishonor" tattoo-designs.

Tattoos openly admitting and even extolling their perver-

* There have been cases, however rare, where women of the more respectable strata had similar tattooings in similar physical areas. The late Elmer Getchell once reported that a society woman ordered her husband's portrait tattooed upon her breast.

sion are more frequent among male homosexuals. The symbolism is usually quite blatant and is often highly ingenious, with a touch of cynical humor. The designs are frequently considered as effective excitants. One sailor boasted on his back a pack of hounds engaged in a serious chase after a rabbit. The rabbit's hind legs only are visible; the rest of him has apparently disappeared into a handy and logical burrow. Active pederasts naturally concentrate their tattooings on their active sexual organs.

The process of such tattooing is often connected with autoeroticism. An American seaman bought a tattooing set from a Bowery master, and shortly thereafter appeared displaying his virile organs tattooed in blue, black, green and red. Of decoration used for the purpose of sexual allure this is perhaps one of the flashier examples.

3

With some of the American seamen visiting Japan tattooing was a frankly masochistic experience. There, in the beginning of this century, many of the tattooers were not men, but young girls. They had an increasingly larger volume of trade than men-tattooers—for the same reason that there appeared in the American Far West, within the last decade or so, a number of women-barbers.*

Some of these Japanese girl-tattooers also practised prosti-

* In Algeria, at one time, women were the professional tattooers, and stood in the market place offering their skill. Up till lately the best known tattooer in the sailors' quarters of Norfolk, Va., was a woman. During the late war Burchett, the London tattooer, had a young woman assistant, and his shop was crowded with what he characteristically called "patients," both English and American. At the same time American sailors and soldiers gave generous custom to a French lass in Bordeaux, daughter of a sailor-tattooer lost at sea in the sinking of a French submarine. She was as truly masculine and sadistic as her job called for; one of her American customers reports to me that "her needles hurt more than any others and there was soreness for several weeks."

tution. Not infrequently the two acts were combined. As tattooing of the natives was forbidden by the Japanese government many years ago, the Japanese tattooers had to confine their clientele to foreign visitors. Later, about fifteen or twenty years ago, even this trade was restricted. The American tattooers explain this restriction by the fact that the tattooing of foreign visitors in Japan had become so overwhelmingly and openly sexual. The tattooers tell me that after this restriction many of the girl-tattooers migrated to the Philippines and Hawaii where they continued their trade in the same fashion. One of the most representative examples of such tattooing is a Japanese resident of Ithaca, New York. On the most unlikely places he has butterflies, birds, flies, spiders and centipedes, all very miniature, tattooed with considerable skill. He is an exhibitionist with a definite passive homosexuality: on his occasional trips to New York, he visits a Bowery tattooer to whom again and again he displays his tattooing and fondly recalls the strong masculine girl back in Yokohama who did the job. To him the Bowery tattooman is a counterpart of the Yokohama girl.

IV

the youth

1

If your janitor's children take to pen and ink, and draw wrist-watches on their wrists, faces on their finger-nails, rings around their fingers, and circles around their knuckles, the chances are that by the time they are fifteen they will find their way to the waterfront, there to acquire a tattooed snake on the arm or a butterfly on the thigh. The venerable tattoo establishments of America now depend for custom on the callow landlubbing adolescents rather than on the sailors. See them come to the shops, young East Siders, in groups of three or four,—there is your herd-motive in tattooing. See their puny, undersized figures,—there is your inferiority-motive, the desire to attain manliness and strength through the pain of the tattoo-wound, to identify themselves with some worshipped adult.

A former sailor obtained a job in the shipping room of a film company in New York. Soon he was running things not only in that particular shipping room but in the back-offices of many other companies of the film center. He was masterly—he knew how to fix things and people—he was power personified. On his right arm was the tattooed design of an Indian maiden. As shipping work is shirt-sleeve work, the tattoo was visible. A young quiet boy in the office was drawn by the ex-sailor's personality. He tried to become close to the man, flattered him, sought his protection, and succeeded. Now he lost his reserve, swaggered, swore, was boisterous. One day he did not report for work. The next day he appeared, the sleeve covering his right hand. In a few days he rolled the sleeve back. There was the large tattooed design of an Indian girl, an exact replica of the ex-sailor's ornament. It was identification of a weak youngster with a strong adult. It was a form of totemism. The Indian girl of the ex-sailor's arm was to the younger boy a magic design, not only a mark but also a cause of manliness.

Isolated cases of the tattooing of minors in America have been reported in the press ever since P. T. Barnum's tattooed Greek excited the imagination and the libidos of parents. For, up to the beginning of this century, most frequently it was not the minors themselves who set out to be tattooed. It was the parents who expressed their sadistic or incestuous impulses by tattooing their children, ostensibly for purposes of identification (against loss or kidnapping) or commercial exhibition. But beginning with the early 1900's it was the children themselves who found their way to the tattooers. They found them easily because by that time there were many more tyro-tattooers than there were places for them in established tattoo-shops. The tyros needed live skin upon which to rehearse their newly-acquired art. Children of New York's East Side were a real convenience.

When the East Side schools opened in the fall of 1902 the teachers were amazed at the number of tattooed youngsters. The boys explained that they had been tattooed during the preceding summer. Feeling, perhaps, that it was none of their affair, the teachers took no action, even after the boys who until then had remained free of decorations began to emulate their comrades.

Nor were most of the parents perturbed to any noticeable degree. But presently a Jewish father burst in with a complaint. He wouldn't have minded the decorations on his boy's chest had it not been for the fact that one of the designs was a crucifix. An indignant mother came from her Attorney Street tenement wailing that a tattooer had pricked her boy's skin with an extensive cemetery scene, inscribed: "To the Memory of Beloved Mother Gone to Rest." Just about this time a dozen smaller boys and even girls trooped in, their faces decorated with butterflies, beetles, shrimps and lobsters. Here was a primitive artistic impulse allied with the herd-emulation motif. The teachers, now in a panic, called in the Society for the Prevention of Cruelty to Children.

Agent King investigated. He found that the latest facial decorations on the children were not tattooings but the result of the application of transfer-paper figures. These were removed after a few washings. However, enough real tattooings were found on the skins of the boys to cause the arrest of a Bowery tattooer. He was brought to court but released after promising to keep his needles and pigments away from young boys.

The next court case in connection with the tattooing of minors occurred in the fall of 1906, when the same Mr. King, of the same Society, found on the Bowery a girl of fifteen, freshly tattooed, in the company of two sailors. As the boy in the film office signified his sexual awakening by an identification with the ex-sailor, so this girl acquired tattoos as the symbol of her sexual dawn. She was the daughter of a prosperous produce merchant; she had disappeared from her Brooklyn home some three weeks earlier. When apprehended by Mr. King she averred that she was in love with navy life, that she planned to don male attire and enlist as a sailor, thus betraying a strong masculine tendency, a streak of revolt against her own sex. Three tattooers of the Bowery who had decorated her with designs were arrested and held in $100 bail each for violation of a section of the Penal Code which makes it a misdemeanor "to endanger the life, health or morals of a minor child." No prison sentences for the tattooers resulted from these arrests.

Besides New York, a number of other states frown upon the tattooing of minors and take measures against it. The general attitude is expressed in a statement once made by a probation officer in the State of Washington: "If a man wishes to take such punishment as tattooing, it is none of our business, but to make a spectacle of a child is more than we will endure." In Washington measures against the tattooing of minors were taken after a child had fainted twice while undergoing the operation in a Spokane penny arcade.

In New York, as well as in a number of other states, the tattooers make a show of complying with the law. On the walls of their shops they hang signs to the effect that no minors under eighteen years will be tattooed unless accompanied by a parent. However, almost any youngster over fourteen can get himself tattooed, even if he has no parent with him. It is no exaggeration to say that most of the present-day tattoo-custom in America is supplied by boys under twenty, and a considerable part of these are well under eighteen.

Frederick C. Helbing, Superintendent of the House of Refuge on Randall's Island, New York, states that twenty percent of the boy-inmates are found to be tattooed when received in the institution. The reception age limit at the present time is nineteen, but until July 1, 1932, it was eighteen. The boys come not from the city of New York alone, but from all over the state, and there are tattooed boys even among those who come from inland and rural points. When questioned, they say that they got tattooed "just for fun," or "because the other boys in the gang did it," or that they didn't know why. So far, all but one have confessed that they were sorry they had submitted to the process and now would like to have the decorations removed. The one exception, an Italian boy, said: "Why do you think I spent my money on this? Only to take it off?" I would not place any special credence in the "shame" and "sorrow" and willingness to have the tattoos removed as voiced by the other boys. Probably many of them sensed the disapproval of the officials and framed their answers accordingly.*

2

Get the youths to talk at their ease. Before they know what they are doing they will betray that, with many of them, tattooing has a deep sexual significance.

Here is the case of P.E., a youth of meagre education and restricted social background. Discussing the two figures tattooed on his arms (a boxer on the right arm, a girl on the left), he said:

> I was tattooed at the age of 18. I went down with some fellows to the Bowery—Charlie Wagner's place. They were getting tattooed and they said, you are yellow—you are afraid—come and get tattooed. I said I wasn't afraid

* With the most commendable sincerity, Mr. Helbing has been instrumental in the recent introduction, by New York State Senator Mandelbaum, of a bill amending Paragraph 483 of the Penal Code punishing those who endanger a minor's life, health or morals. The proposed amendment, to be known as Paragraph 483c, is to prohibit, expressly, the tattooing of a child under sixteen. It reads: "A person who marks the body of a child under the age of sixteen years, with indelible ink or pigments, is guilty of a misdemeanor." There is a possibility that in its final version the bill will raise the age limit to 18 and even perhaps to 21. But the passing of the bill, as with every other American law, does not, of course, mean its thorough enforcement. The usual run of political appointees, entrusted with this province, will bungle or, at best, neglect it as completely as they do every other law. As a matter of fact Paragraph 483, even unamended, could be sufficient to halt the tattooing of minors were its enforcement detailed as a task of some enlightened social-work organization, and not of the ordinary run of police.

> but I was a little frightened. When I saw those needles and everything I got scared. I did it because I didn't want to be a coward. When I got home my father gave me a licking for it. It wasn't more than three weeks after that I wanted to have them removed. I am ashamed now to have them on my arm. When you meet decent people or go out in society, people think you are a roustabout and rowdy and it goes against you. I would give anything to take it off. I wanted to run away from the place as soon as I was finished. I didn't feel comfortable there.
>
> I had a feeling something like that when I first had intercourse. Some fellow says he wanted to break me in and took me to a whore on the East Side. I didn't know what it was about. I was very much ashamed. The woman showed me how to do it. When it was finished, I couldn't stay there. I felt like running away. It was something like the feeling I had when I was tattooed.

Commenting on this and similar cases, Dr. Bromberg observes that through the reactions of such youths, one obtains a clearer understanding of the inner significance of tattoo markings to the individual. It is plain that the defense reactions which are forthcoming soon after the design is put on are the recoil of the individual from a situation menacing his social integrity and security. The dim awareness of the significance of the tattooing already becomes evident as soon as the episode is over.

Dr. Bromberg points to another case of a muscular, vigorous man of twenty-five who had had the figure of a war nurse tattooed on his arm at the age of eighteen, and who stated that it was done in company with a crowd who "sort of forced me into it." It was almost a seduction and it is from this implied homosexual seduction that the ego of the average young man recoils. It is especially patent, says Dr. Bromberg, when the tattooing is done under the influence of alcohol. He cites the case of a youth who, at the age of sixteen, while in the navy, was tattooed in Shanghai in the company of an equally intoxicated shipmate. The youth said that the next day when he had recovered from the spree he regretted what he had done.

Dr. Bromberg notes: "When we go deeper into the study of the meaning of the guilt feeling found in tattooed subjects, we come upon what the Freudians call the castration complex." This castration fear is an infantile situation carried throughout the boy's life, a dread that the father will punish him for his sexual activities. In his early fantasies, say the Freudians, the use of the child's phallus as a rival of his father's for the love of the mother becomes punishable by a revengeful father: the only adequate revenge for such tabooed* desire is the deprivation of the phallus, the castration by the father. The remorse and fear engendered by masturbation in most boys are but a representation of this early castration fear.**

There are many things in the tattooing situation that suggest these factors as the operative ones. In the first place the tattooer is an older man who through the symbolized needle and tattooing fluid enters into a suggestive relationship with the youth. A young soldier told me that his father "raised Zion" when he returned from the service with some tattoos

* It is significant that *taboo* and *tattoo* are the only two Polynesian words that have wide usage in the English language, as well as in a number of other white man's languages, and that both words were introduced at about the same time.

** This fear of castration found for itself a singular illustration in the case of Tom Poole, of Greenville, South Carolina, who sprang from the operating table and attacked his surgeon. He said he was offended because the surgeon, while operating on him for a minor illness, slashed a tattooed American flag. Tom Poole threatened to bring the doctor to the courts. His rationalization of his action by the pseudo-motive of patriotism does not conceal the true reason—his fear of castration closely bound up with the tattooing.

on his arms; the father, a physician, took infinite trouble to remove the tattooing from the arms. A similarly characteristic illustration of a father's jealousy we find in Captain William Barnes' book, *When Ships Were Ships and Not Tin Pots,** where the Captain says: "I have only a few little tattoos on me, a few little spots on my hands and a half of an anchor on the muscle of my left arm, which would have been finished, only I got a heavy kick on the backside from my father which landed me across the floor on my head and the anchor never got finished." The Captain's father, as well as the young soldier's father-physician and many other fathers who protest against their boys' tattooings, may be incredulous and indignant if told that their rage is really sexual jealousy. The fathers are incensed not at the barbarism of the operation but, however little they suspect it, at the homosexual, seductive elements of it. Darkly they feel as if the tattooers had raped their sons.

It is said of certain American tattooers that they betray their homosexual cravings by the way they hold the young boys' arms and legs while tattooing them—not by the double finger pressure customary in tattooing but by the more intimate full grasp of their hands. While tattooing young boys they delay far longer than the operation calls for. In the old times of prosperity when the shops were thronged these masters would pick out of the waiting crowd not the mature men who had money and were thus better customers but young adolescents who were not likely to have money.

Again, says Dr. Bromberg, tattooing is often done when the subject is under the influence of liquor, and it is well known in clinical psychiatry that drinking releases latent homosexual tendencies. Indeed, the adolescent chumming represents, according to the Freudians, this tendency. Almost always the young tattoo subject goes to a tattoo master

* New York: Albert & Charles Boni, 1930.

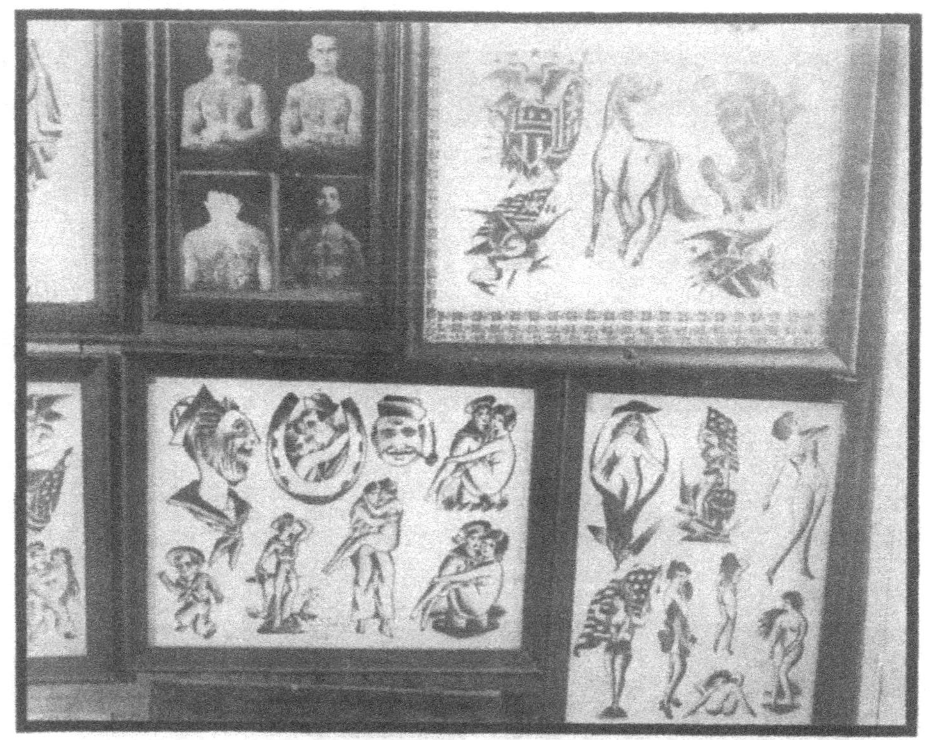

Sample tattooers' show-cards, giving some idea of the variety of the designs.

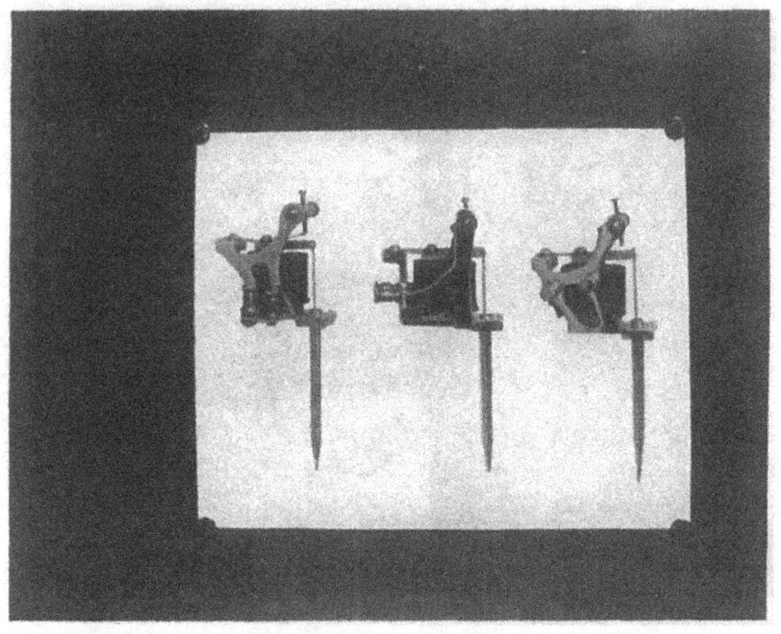

Tattoo by Electricity
The modern electric tattoo tool, capable of making about three thousand jabs a minute.

with other friends. His very reluctance indicates that the sense of guilt is operating. His ego fears the anticipated punishment for a perverse activity. He is uneasy and not seldom frightened. "One of our cases reports a feeling of panic and a desire to flee."

It is clear to see the origin, in this type of youth, of the fear they have of offending people. One boy said: "When I go on the beaches among decent people it looks funny." Another, already quoted: "When you go among people it looks vulgar, they think you're a rowdy."

To trace the relationship between the castration complex and the individual and the fear reaction toward the superego would take us too deeply into theoretic psychoanalysis, but without this explanation it is impossible to understand certain aspects of the psychology of tattooing, the headlong flight, the overwhelming anxieties that boys develop after they have been tattooed. Certainly this disgust is too powerful to arise from the conscious layers of the mind; tattooing is too shot through with the symbolism of sexuality to have no relation to the unconscious fear that is represented in every man by the castration complex. These who have seen many young men with tattoo markings and who have questioned them have invariably observed a gesture of a wiping off of the tattoo mark from the skin.

However, it would be a mistake to suppose that all or most of the young men suffer from this guilt complex consciously, that all or most wish to have the tattooings removed. I repeat that many of the guilt-answers given by the boys and youths in clinical and penal institutions are dictated not by their own conscious attitudes but by their desire to find favor in the eyes of the doctors and other officials who question them, and whose unfavorable attitude to the tattooing they immediately sense.

The guilt-complex is not universal. As Dr. Bromberg

rightly points out, two outstanding prototypes may be distinguished in the survey of types of individuals who are tattooed. One type is represented by the virile, muscular man —often a sailor or truckman. He is an outdoor man; he carries his tattoos in a proud, yet nonchalant manner that bespeaks his satisfaction with them. The professional tattooer and the exhibitor are at the extreme left wing of this group. They are covered with tattooings and continue to increase them from year to year. The other type is a young man, a city dweller who has had brief contact with the army or navy, whose tattooings were made in the rashness of his youth as a gesture toward strength and masculine recognition, and are regretted throughout his life. For this youth the tattooings remain the sign of momentary weakness; for the other it is the sign of his strength. Almost everywhere in large cities one can find the second group, usually in the lower social stratum. The first type wears his markings proudly, they are for him a constant gratification of his narcissism; the second wears his designs with an uneasiness that indicates his atonement for the adolescent flight into narcissism, which now hangs like an albatross around his neck.

V

the art and its masters

1

Stop and ponder on the many American tattoo designs. At first they may seem crude and primitive. They have no greatness. But soon you discover a certain charm in their line, and this impression once acquired never leaves you. For you discover the spirit of art as understood and enjoyed by the folk-masses of America: the sailors, the soldiers, the day-laborers, the farm-hands, the cowboys, the miners, the loggers, the hoboes—and their sweethearts and sometimes wives. The tattoo-medium caters to their feeling for primitive pathos and simple sentimentality.

See this blue sailor kneeling down before a red tombstone, his head dolefully bare and bent, one hand clutching his hat, the other holding a dark-green flower. Read the inscription on the tombstone: "My Dear Mother." What mother-bereft seaman could withstand the inevitable temptation of ordering this fresco to be etched on his brave chest, next to the customary crucifix "Rock of Ages," which, as is well known, protects the tar from all general mishaps? Regard these pigs and roosters which seamen have engraved on their feet—grand and sure-working precaution against drowning. You will also marvel at a bit of sea with the protruding masts of a sunken ship, the whole tableau explained in a black-lettered title: "A Sailor's Grave," or: "The Sailor's Last Port." You can also witness a tattooer's talent exhibiting itself in the lively picture of a sailor dancing a jig on a gigantic anchor, or in daggers with ribbons inscribed determinedly: "Death Before Dishonor"; in fanciful horseshoes lettered: "Good Luck"; in a human skull and crossbones framed in the terrible-looking circle of a snake; mirth-provoking "Happy Hooligans"; awe-inspiring angels; naked ladies strangled by snakes; alluring girls occupying a spider's place in a spider web—a thoughtful reminder to any embittered lover; reckless female rope-dancers; Indian girls; cow-girls; pirate girls; jockey girls; and many other girls of various races and occupations. There are also all kinds of birds, animals, fish and legendary monsters, such as dragons, devil-satyrs and sundry sea-beasts. All are startling, tempting, beckoning to any plain-souled American lover of this homely, half-savage art.

Whence come these motifs?

The religious tattooings can be easily traced to the hoary times of the early Christians of England, and of the pilgrims returning from the Holy Land with holy designs tattooed upon them.

The grotesque flora and fauna designs are of distinct Oriental origin, having been brought to America by P. T. Barnum's freak, Captain Constantine, whose career is fully treated in a later chapter. His influence was reinforced by the American sailors and society-folk bringing home dainty Japanese tattooings. Later, English tattooers such as Sutherland Macdonald took up the Oriental style, dwelling on the careful detail of the roses, dragons, spiders in the webs, peacocks and their tails. Since the 1890's they have been bitterly complaining that the Oriental style is being ruined by the rough work of the American tattooers. The American masters reply that they can't help it, that the American plebs care not for dainty detail, that the order is for a big splash at a small expense in a jiffy.

The love and patriotism designs are of uniquely American origin. American sailors used them in the early days of the republic to express their sentiments, and, allegedly, to provide means of identification in cases of drowning or of mortal battle wounds. Each new war created new designs. The Civil War left its record of tattooed pictures of victorious Monitors and mottoes extolling the Union. The Spanish-American conflict boosted pictures of steam-battleships crowding out the sailships hitherto overwhelmingly popular among the tattoo-fans; the World War brought in its wake tattooed representations of airplanes and aviators, also pictures of Red Cross girls with the inscription: "Rose of No Man's Land."

The birth of the newspaper comic strip found its reflection in the orders for tattooed replicas of Mutt and Jeff, Jiggs and Maggie, Pop-Eye, the Katzenjammer Kids, Felix the Cat, and the like. New popular phrases such as "So's your old man,"* were imprinted on the skin shortly after they were coined. The movies brought a batch of orders for the portraits of favorite actors and actresses, including Rin-Tin-Tin, to be duplicated on the biceps and shoulders. The latest wrinkles are Marlene Dietrich and Mickey Mouse. Mickey, having become a folk character, will probably outlast Marlene. The war-time fad of tattooing pictures of airplanes and airmen was revived in the middle 1920's, the sensation of Lindbergh's flight across the Atlantic serving as a tremendous impetus. Thousands of tattoo-addicts rushed to the needlemen and ordered designs of airplanes inscribed "The

* An illustration accompanied by a So's-your-old-man inscription was ordered from Frank Graf by a sailor. It was the picture of a monkey hanging from a tree by its tail. The sailor's own idea.

Spirit of St. Louis," also tattooed portraits of young airmen more or less resembling Lindbergh.

It is the customers and not the masters who are really responsible for new fashions. The American tattoo-masters remain, on the whole, a slow and unprogressive lot. Most of their designs are old and crude. On their own initiative they rarely add anything new or sensational. Their wall-boards and window-displays still abound in the archaic styles of the 1890's and 1900's. If a new touch is wanted the customer is expected to bring a magazine cover, a movie star's photo, or a comic clipping.

2

No one knows just how many tattooers there are in the United States. Estimates vary from several hundred to two thousand. The latter figure may be close to the truth if we include the numerous amateurs who, having purchased sets from mail-order tattoo-firms, now practise in their off-hours on themselves and on their friends, finding payment in the pleasure of it.

Most of our professional tattooers are native Americans, though you will occasionally find one of Jewish or Italian descent. The few Japanese tattooers at one time assisting in a New York shop are gone these twenty-five or thirty years, but in New Orleans even to this day you will find several Chinese masters. Most of the professional tattooers make their headquarters in ports, or in such large centers of migratory workers as Chicago and Detroit, or in army-concentration cities like San Antonio.

Their shops, with a few notable exceptions, are small and dirty. They themselves are, on the whole, clean-shaven and quiet-spoken men, younger-looking than their age. Most of them used to exhibit their own tattooed bodies in circuses, dime-museums, county-fairs and carnivals, and they are fond of recalling the old days on the wheel. They tend to be jealous of their reputations as artists. Rarely do they praise another master's work; they seldom hobnob with each other. They accuse each other of being a "jagger," a trade term for a man who does not use his own designs or free-hand methods, who employs stencils, is careless of detail and of sanitary conditions. They are nationalists to a man. They will tell you that a few years back Billy Donnelly made a trip into the interior of New Zealand, but returned disgusted, saying that the art of skin-puncture was dying out in its native home and that the West—America and England—was destined to carry on and improve upon the glorious work. "Electric" Elmer Getchell argued that the tattooer's art should be ranked with music, poetry and painting. Dr. Bromberg states:

> There is no question that the professional tattooer is in some way peculiar. He considers himself a master, an "artist." It is known that in the underworld a homosexual is also called an "artist." His associates are of the periphery of society; the prostitutes and ne'er-do-wells who are tattooed belong here. The tattooing represents a sort of perverse sexual act; such persons are apt to become part of a special exclusive world, very much like homosexuals who live and travel in an esoteric circle. The professional tattooer (or circus exhibitor) is very proud of his skill as well as of his fortitude in being able to stand the pain involved. He speaks in an offhand manner of the pain when one asks him about it.

Yet I know some tattooers who scorn their own calling, good craftsmen though they may be. Bitterly they grumble, once you have their confidence, about the base rabble who come to them to be "covered," about the bad times now smiting the tattoo-craft. They explain that they got into the game years ago, being young and foolish, and that it is too late now to do anything about it. With a truly masochistic delight they denounce tattoo and themselves.

The earliest recorded professional tattooer in America was Martin Hildebrandt. Certainly he was the first American tattooer to cease his hoboing around the country, his ink in a clamshell, and to open a permanent shop. (O'Reilly later claimed this priority, but he was wrong.) In the middle 1870's Hildebrandt had what he called an atelier in Oak Street, between Oliver and James Streets, New York. He said he had been in this business ever since 1846, and he relished the memory of the Civil War, during which he had never had a moment's idle time. "I must have marked thousands of sailors and soldiers," he boasted in later years. "I am pretty well known all over the United States." Like every tattooer since his days he claimed to have had trained all the other masters in the country and sadly shook his head over the imperfect lines they have been turning out since they left him. "Now there is Lee of Philadelphia, a left-handed man, a pupil of mine, but I regret to say his work is none of the best." When Hildebrandt admitted the existence of a genius outside his own atelier, it was always in the past tense. In Chicago, he said, there used to be a man whose real name was Farrell, a former West Pointer, who did wonderfully fine work, but he took to drinking and lost his skill.

Hildebrandt remained discreetly silent about Samuel F. O'Reilly, then a young man but a rising star in the profession. O'Reilly settled in New York in 1875. For his location he selected the spot where Chatham Square gives birth to the Bowery—at the very mouth of the Thieves' Highway.

O'Reilly was the first to use the electric process of tattooing, speeding up the work enormously, and coining a fortune for himself in the course of a few years. He called tattoos "tattaugraphs." Such well-known figures as Ed Smith and

Charlie Wagner were trained by him. He elevated the craft by calling himself Professor, generously bestowing the same rank upon his apprentices. He expanded the choice of materials till it included such old and new stuff as powdered charcoal, finely powdered brick-dust, coal-dust, lamp black, Prussian blue, washing blue, gunpowder, cinnabar, ordinary writing ink, China ink, India ink, and other vegetable inks. He frowned upon the belief that mother's milk shot through a needle would remove tattooing or that urine would do the job even better. He introduced a good chemical for the removal. But he and Electric Elmer lapsed into the error of court litigation over their patent rights, dropping their electric-tattoo profits into the avid palms of lawyers. In 1908, weary and heartsore, Professor O'Reilly died as a result of an accident. He fell off a ladder, while painting his home in Brooklyn. A Sophoclean death.

O'Reilly's electric tattoo-tool was a hollow ink reservoir feeding a set of needles. After the bared part of the body was shaved and washed, an oiled paper with an outline of a design was placed on the skin, and a tracing made. A true artist made a free-hand tracing, scorning oiled papers or any other stencils. Then the electric needle was applied, much in the manner of a sewing-machine needle, along the traced lines. Next came the coloring and shading. A triple or quadruple needle was used for this; the pricking was sharper. One saw only a shapeless spot or series of spots; the ink seemed to run all over the wound without following the lines of the design. In fact, the ink penetrated the skin only where the skin was punctured. The design was seen clearly after the local area had been rubbed with oil and washed with witch hazel. Within the next six or seven days there was an inflammation. A scale formed, fell away, revealed the design in its clear finality.

In the modern electric method the dry coloring pigment is mixed with water, alcohol, cocoa oil, or saliva. The black color alone comes ready made as an ink. The needles are most often dipped in these inks or mixtures. Another method, that of spreading the pigment over the skin and puncturing the skin through the pigment, is used less frequently. Still another method, moistening the needles with saliva and then dipping them into the dry pigment, is the rarest of all.

The electric machine is capable of making about three thousand jabs a minute as against one hundred and fifty to two hundred jabs of the hand tool. It has been somewhat improved since O'Reilly's days. It is less bulky and works by vibration instead of the old rotary motor. Now its shape resembles that of a pistol, the butt being formed by two electric coils, the barrel containing a needle bar, which ends in a group of small, fine, steel needles. The needles vibrate upward and downward. They seldom draw blood, puncturing the skin no deeper than one thirty-second of an inch, or even one sixty-fourth. The sensation of the pricking is that of a slight burn or at most a mosquito bite. Two machines are used in every tattooing process of today: the outline puncher, holding from two to four needles, and the filler, holding from six to twelve needles. Some of the tattooing pigments and liquids used today are manufactured in this country, but German chemical concerns seem to have a more active interest in the field and offer a more thorough service. A recent German catalogue listed no less than seventeen shades of different tattooing colors. But even the Germans do little to improve the tattoo-tools. "Dad" Liberty, the Boston tattooer, talks of inventing a new electric machine that would eliminate the present vibration, noise and pain, and cause pleasant, smooth, throbbing strokes. But, so far, one regrets to state, it has been only talk.

3

In the early 1900's, after the general acceptance of the electric tools, the tattoo-business boomed. Master-tattooers began to advertise heavily in the *Police Gazette* and the *Billboard*, offering mail-order machines, supplies, designs and instruction to aspiring amateurs. Somebody discovered that skilful tattooers could camouflage, with whitish ink, any sort and size of black eye. It became a good side-line, and remained so until Prohibition, when drugstores began to compete by selling a special medicinal paint to the heroes of speakeasy combats. Another side-line was discovered, and proved of longer life, when girls and women came with their beauty spot-and-blush orders.

The beginning of the century witnessed the rise of Lew-the-Jew, a former wall-paper designer. Beauty is only skin deep, and Lew discovered the truth of this axiom to his delight, surprise and life-long fascination in the far-off Philippines. He shipped himself to those isles in the now half-forgotten days of hoochee-coochee, horseless carriages, and McKinley's anti-Spanish crusade. He fought the Spaniards bravely and well, and, along with dysentery, contracted the tattoo-craze.

Lew did not stop at having a few choice pictures punctured into his own epidermis. He decided to try his skill on others, and soon Admiral Dewey and Lew-the-Jew were running a neck-and-neck race for fame among the army and navy. When Lew was discharged he carried away with him the good-will of thousands of soldiers, sailors and marines whom he had tattooed. Customers, military and civilian, were waiting for him in the States, where his newly acquired distinction preceded him. Forgotten was the wall paper trade.

The turn of the century was a most opportune time for a

capable young man to start in the tattoo business. The Spanish War had sent out to sea a large number of Americans who returned home with a few tattoo-designs on their chests, backs, arms and legs, as the tradition of the sea decreed, and an itching for more pictures to add to their galleries. The invention of the electric tattoo-machine had, by the late 1890's, supplanted the slow old hand-method and facilitated the execution of increased orders. Instead of days, the process now took hours. Most tattoo-masters were so overwhelmed by business that they had no time to think up new patterns. Yet, more than ever before, new patterns were much needed, because the greater number of new customers called for a wider variety of selections.

Lew-the-Jew came to the rescue. He had preserved his original freshness of attitude. Tattooing was as yet an art, not a mere trade to him. He spent his days at his electric needles tattooing multitudes of bodies of all conditions, ages and social positions. He dedicated his nights to creating and drawing his designs. Hundreds of tattoo-masters in all American ports and many inland points snapped up Lew's patterns. To this day many tattoo-shops use them for at least fifty percent of their business. That is why so much American tattooing looks like the walls of your grandmother's living-room. Lew-the-Jew preeminently left his mark on the folk-art of America.

In the first quarter of this century the following lights shone the brightest in the ranks of American tattooists: Lew-the-Jew, Charlie Wagner, and Electric Elmer Getchell in New York; "Old Dutch" in Chicago; Buckee in Philadelphia; Harry V. Lawson and Gus Wagner in Los Angeles; G. Kreuger in Seattle; Joe Lieber and Louis Morgan in San Francisco; Eddie Poferl in Minneapolis; "Red" Gibbons in San Antonio and St. Louis; Lenora Platt in Norfolk, the

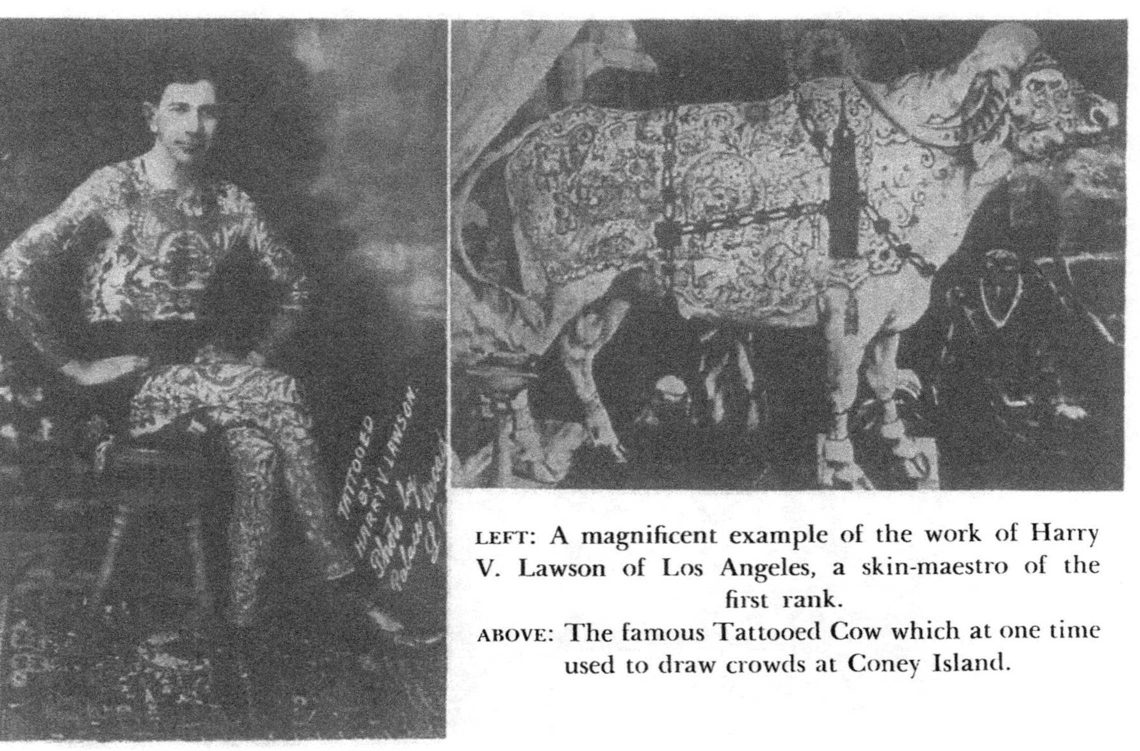

LEFT: A magnificent example of the work of Harry V. Lawson of Los Angeles, a skin-maestro of the first rank.

ABOVE: The famous Tattooed Cow which at one time used to draw crowds at Coney Island.

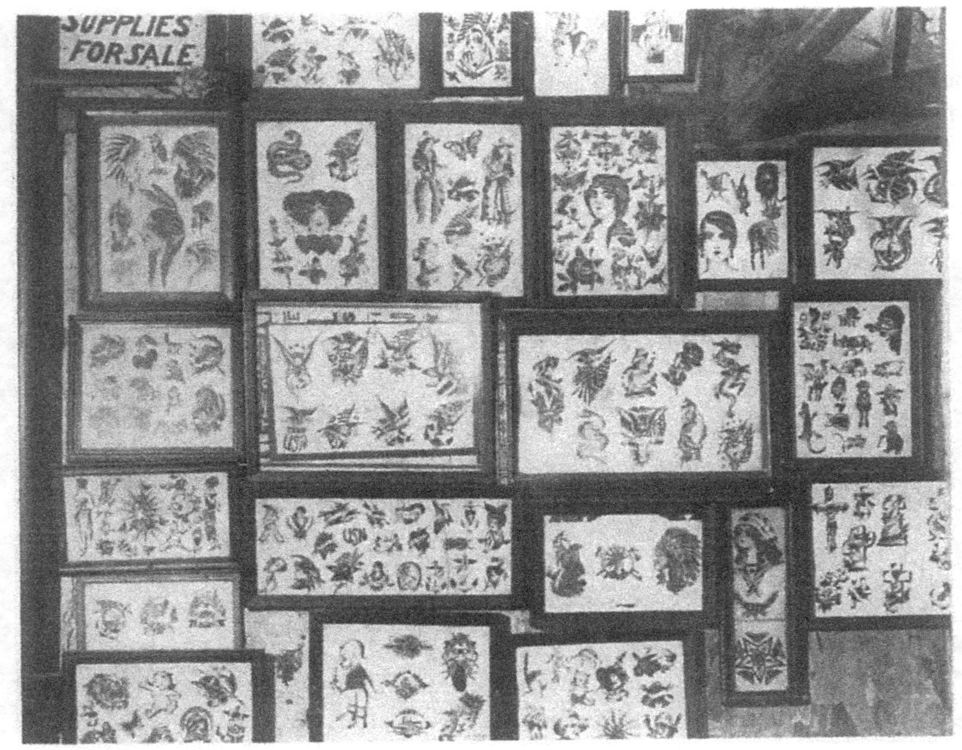

More sample-charts. Observe the conventionality of most of the designs.

most famous woman-tattooer in this country; Dad E. W. Liberty in Boston; George Pennell in New Orleans.

"Old Dutch," up to his death in the middle 1920's, held electric tools in horror, as a desecration of his art. Red Gibbons is considered even by latter-day connoisseurs as the best artist in the profession, comparable to the finest Japanese tattooers of the 1890's. Harry V. Lawson was, up until the recent darkness of the depression, one of the swankiest of the masters. He kept a three-room establishment, consisting of a reception room, an operating room, and a rest room. On his desk-top there was a display of bulky medical volumes. On the walls, framed in neat wood and glass, were samples of tattooed human skin, taken from corpses. This never failed to bring Harry publicity from the Los Angeles newspapers, and he loved it. None of the New York masters, not even Wagner—shark for publicity though he is—can point to any such display on his studio walls. This may be explained by the fact that in New York the supply of tattooed human skin is cornered by a certain gentleman of leisure who collects the samples for a hobby, as one would collect cigar-labels or old Americana. He knows a first-rate tattoo when he sees one, approaches the bearer, and signs an agreement with him in re skin-delivery after the man's death. This gentleman also manipulates a dissecting-room monopoly. He is without doubt the only living human with a constant corner in epithelia.

Harry Lawson would never divulge his technique of securing the skin (perhaps, it was no more sinister than taking the smaller designs off live bodies through surgery). Instead he would shift the conversation to his aristocratic clientele. He would tell you that some of our most exalted citizens—lawyers, bankers, corporation directors—have the tattoo-habit in their souls and the most stunning tattoo-marks on their hides. One of his best customers was a doctor of medicine who had his entire body punctured with the most fantastic pictures ending in the prettiest bands you ever saw around his wrists and ankles. "And him being a very educated and high-minded chap, yessir! Why, he's a thirty-third degree Mason, yessir, a thirty-third! Why, there was a fine, large, intelligent, high-class lady down to my shop the other day. Had the Eastern Star tattooed right on her left hip."

Similarly Owen Jensen, who at one time worked for Harry Lawson, boasted to me that once he had tattooed a governor of Colorado. The same desire to prove their art genteel forces Lawson, Jensen and other tattooers to memorize long lists of the tattooed royalty of England, Sweden, and other lands. But the fact that the royalty of the western world goes in for tattooing did not save even Lawson from losing his fine three-room studio after the depression set in, and from reverting to the same sort of hole in the wall as is the fate of all other American tattooers. Gone are the war times when a deft American tattooer was raking in from $75 to $100 a day, the needles zooming feverishly to supply the hundreds of thousands of new army and navy recruits with images of Red Cross nurses, half-naked Columbias, Statues of Liberty, eagles, dragons, horseshoes, and other fitting designs. In those days you had to arrange for an appointment with a tattooer as you would with a Park Avenue physician—days and weeks in advance. Gone are the post-war days when flocks of girls fluttered into the tattoo-shops to get their artificial beauty spots, permanent blushes, eternal ruby-lips, as well as tiny flowers, kewpie-dolls, united hearts, and such. Charlie Wagner, for the first time in the alleged forty-three years of his puncturing experience, may now be seen in front of his shop in an actual endeavor to pull in potential customers. It is a bitter pass for the tattooer's art when it has to resort to the methods of the cheap clothier next door. Charlie is currently reported to have dropped some eleven thousand dollars, his life-savings, in the Wall Street débâcle of 1929. They say that often he has to go without breakfast until his first customer leaves him his fee, and this may be as late as eleven o'clock in the morning or perhaps later. Now Charlie and other tattooers in New York and elsewhere make no more than a bare living. Custom is scarce despite the lowered fees —from two and five dollars down to two and four bits per average design.

4

There are four tattooers in America who even through the depression continue to advertise in national publications and do mail-order business. They are Miller of Norfolk, Sergeant Bonzey of Providence, Percy Waters of Detroit, and William Moore of the Chicago Tattoo Supply House. Their chief medium now is *Popular Mechanics.*

Moore specializes in selling tattoo-removing salves. Bonzey sells by mail not only tattoo-supplies and designs but also crosses and other grave markers. Waters is known for the vitriolic way in which he denounces his competitors. He mails the following leaflet to all who answer his ads:

> FOR YOUR PROTECTION—
> DON'T BE BUNKED
>
> By fly-by-nighters who pose as the largest manufacturers of tattoo supplies in the World. Such jip artists can sell only to the inexperienced buyer. This type of mail order men do not last long, as they depend on catching their customers once. They copy word for word literature put out by others. Designs are also the work of others. They retrace and offer for sale copies from crude photo-

> graphed tracings among which you will find left-hand clasp, rock of ages, woman clinging to left side of cross, Statue of Liberty with left hand up, flags on steamboat waving north, the smoke going south; machines made over from door buzzers, radio parts, tubes made from metallic pencil or umbrella stem. Such crap as this could not be classed with tattooing machines and designs made by a skillful mechanic and artist of long reputation.

None of the New York masters does any mail-order business at this stage of the craft's history, none advertises in the press and mails out leaflets, yet the general consensus of opinion among the American tattoo-fans seems to be that New York, as of old, continues to be the center of the art.

These masters, considering themselves true artists, are restless. They are constantly moving. But being also business men, they do not move away entirely. They simply migrate from one cubicle to another, along the same Park Row-Chatham Square-Bowery line.

At 151 Park Row, at the back of a modernized catchpenny arcade, Frank Graf can be found in the winter. Each spring he moves to a Coney Island dime-museum; last summer he had his sixteenth season doubling as exhibit and practitioner.

In the back-room of a barber-shop at 9 Chatham Square is Bob Wicks, alias "Texas" Bob, condescending about his tattoo-work but enthusiastic about his oil-paintings which now and then he shows and sells at Greenwich Village exhibitions. His real name is Robert Ferraiolo, he was born in Brooklyn of Italian parents, and has never been west of Ohio. He is assisted by Andy Sturtz, who used to follow the fleet from Norfolk to Newport and back and is full of sea lore. Andy is favorably known for the large Buffalo Bill on horseback occupying his entire back.

At 11 Chatham Square, in the dim recesses of a barbershop, is Wagner's tattoo-studio. This is where O'Reilly's studio for many years was located. Charlie has been in business for about thirty years but always adds an extra decade, evidently counting some of O'Reilly's years of work as his own. Until a few months ago, Number 11 was occupied by "Lame" Leroy, a tattooer who as a side-line ran a lunch-counter around the corner. Now Leroy sticks to hash.*

In the tonsorial basement of 12 Bowery is the tattoo-partition of Al Neville, a Welsh soldier and boat-builder, in this country since 1918. He says that as a youth he attended the Birkenhead School of Art, sketching and drawing from models three half-days a week for three years. He learned the tattoo art in Malabar, India, in 1904, but practises it only between major wars and ship-building booms. He says he has never exhibited his own body in circuses or other such enterprises, and does not intend to. He is quietly proud of his service at the French front and the fact that he was wounded while there.

At 16 Bowery is "Sailor" Joe Van Hart, former partner of Charlie Wagner. They now hate each other poisonously.

The last in the line, in the penny-arcade of 42 Bowery near Manhattan Bridge, is Professor Ted, in private life Edgar Hazzard. When business is dull he moodily paints small signs for the hasheries and haberdasheries of the district. In his confidential minutes he hisses: "Smart men don't get tattooed. I'm sorry I'm in this here skin game." The Professor is a little bitter. Recently he disappeared. The other

* Alexander Woollcott recently reported that in Charleston, South Carolina, he saw a sign swinging in front of a shop: "Spaghetti. Light lunches. Tattooing." Thus, Leroy has not been the only food-purveyor in the skin-puncturing business.

tattooers say something about a damage suit as a consequence of a removal job he had done.

Take the bus across the bridge, walk a few paces back, descend into the dark well of Brooklyn's Sands Street. Shades of such famous artists as Billy Donnelly, Jim Wilson, and Lew-the-Jew haunt this fascinating district. But today you will find only one Rembrandt of the needle, Jack Redcloud (the barber-shop at Number 139). Only a few years ago Sands Street was almost riotous with anywhere from four to seven artists. But the depression and the absence of the Navy sent Donnelly back to England, dispatched Wilson to Panama, and Lew-the-Jew to Newark, New Jersey, the other artists disappearing also. The Newark shop keeps on opening and closing indecisively.

It is useless to make a trip to New York's South Street. There the tattooing pursuit is as dead as the two other ancient trades of that street: the making and selling of sails, and the carving of ships' figureheads. Professor Jack was the last permanent artist in this section; no one knows where he is now.* In the summer, an itinerant tattooist may blunder into South Street for a couple of days, try his luck among the listless seamen, and disappear.

The tattooers of New York discuss each other in somewhat ironic terms, though almost all are awed by Bob Wicks and his oil-paintings. Each one has a bright spot in his career of which he is exultantly proud. Graf is intense about a recent summer in Coney Island when he was exhibited and photographed next to Mrs. Jack (Legs) Diamond. He is also proud because he placed six U. S. presidents on the chest of Lady Viola, a circus performer, and a picture of the Capitol on her back, dedicating her arms to the portraits of ten movie

* A report reaches me that in Pittsburgh, in Federal Street, near the Federal Street bridge, a Professor Jack or a Sailor Jack has a tattoo-shop. It may and may not be the Professor of New York's last romantic bit of waterfront.

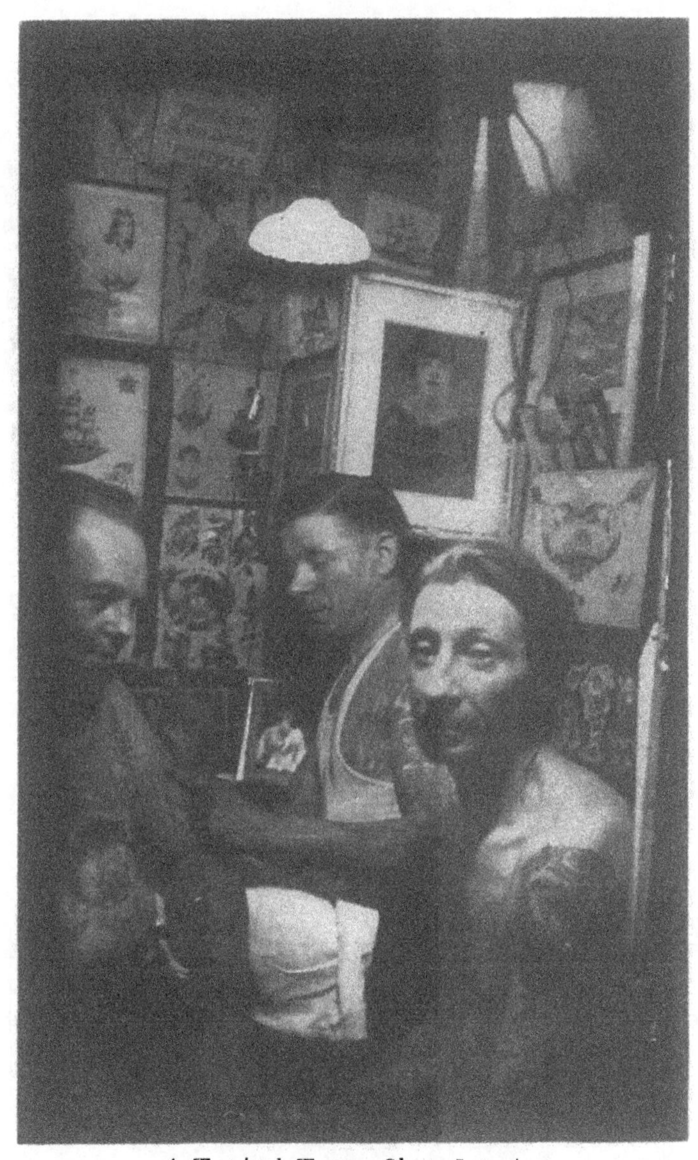

A Typical Tattoo-Shop Interior
Note the profusion of sample-signs on the walls.

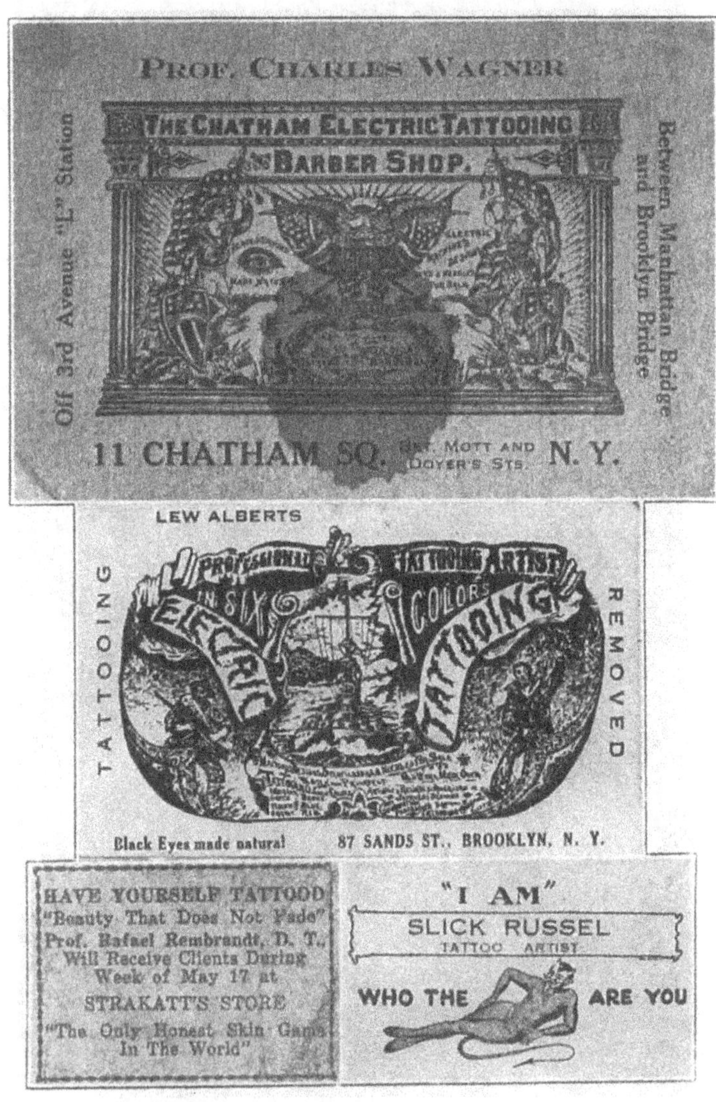

Business cards.

actresses, and her thighs and legs to Babe Ruth, Charlie Chaplin, Tom Mix, Captain Rosenthal of dirigible fame, and other male celebrities. He also cherishes the memory of tattooing, from head to toes, a circus Fat Lady, weight 480 lbs. She afforded more scope to the exercise of his inventive fancy than any other subject he has ever had. Every Christmas eve he sends her, with his compliments of the season, several heavy hunks of ham which she finishes in a day or two, to his never-ending wonder and admiration.

Charlie Wagner waxes voluble over the suicide of Alexander, the Rubber Man, who died of unrequited love for Mae Vandermark and her tattooings.* Wagner is also proud because it was he who tattooed and trained the beautiful Mae, formerly a stenographer in the Plaza Hotel.

Jack Redcloud has his own point of vantage. It is on top of his head—a picture of Christ, in a crown of thorns, tattooed quite artistically. He probably borrowed the idea from a Cuban who once electrified the Bowery by displaying the Cuban national emblem tattooed on his scalp. At that time, in 1925, Jack heard of a juicy contract with a circus which Professor Ted was about to sign. Jack thought that he himself would appreciate a junket around the country. Deciding to beat Professor Ted to the plum, he ordered the picture of Christ onto his head, and, now a stronger attraction than the competitor, won the contract easily. The Professor was irate. Remaining at his Bowery post, he bethought himself of getting a boy-apprentice. He found David Stern, then aged fourteen, the son of a Staten Island lumber dealer and housewrecker. The boy was mad about tattooing, and his mother was indulgent. With her consent David joined Professor Ted, learning the art, and getting tattooed upon his own body. Smarting under the memory of Redcloud's coup, Professor Ted shaved David's pate and tattooed Abraham Lincoln's

* See Chapter VI on the Circus, pages 76-77.

portrait onto it, copying it from a penny. The date of the ceremony was February 12. It was a solemn, patriotic operation, duly photographed for the Professor's ads. David is a strapping young man now, driving a truck for his father in the winter, gravitating back to his tattoo-maestro for the summer.

Each master advertises his skill in his own fashion. Graf has a laconic sign: "Tattooing In Side." Leroy had a special "Tattoo Bulletin Board" with photographs of covered men and women, clippings of magazine and newspaper articles, and such mottoes as: "You want the best doctor why not the same with a tattoo. Walk in." Wicks proclaims: "I Don't care who did the work, or what you paid. I do it Better. I use 6 colors, and charge less for it." Professor Ted emphasizes removal: "I positively have a *sure* tattoo remover Guarantee to remove all color's and ink from the skin. Leaving a smooth Surface. Tattoo Removing Require's about ten to twelve day's No Soreness while having tattoo mark's removed. Leave a Redish Surface eventiouly becoming a natural color."

Charlie Wagner indulges a gift of fancy. His sign reads: "Tat-2-ing." He also has a mannikin figure of a semi-nude tattooed lady in his window. The figure is occasionally hired out for freak millionaire playboy parties. Inside his studio, Wagner has a few framed photostats of Sunday supplement and tabloid stories, with the tattoo as the chief element, horror and sex aplenty. Other frames carry neatly rhymed messages, such as:

By electrical means, without pain,
Your pure epidermis may gain
From head unto heels—
If the idea appeals—
Decorations of which you will be vain.

Business may be slow these difficult times, but the masters

are not discouraged. They estimate that from ten to fifteen percent of American men, and almost five percent of American women, are tattooed. Indeed, Bob Wicks and Jack Redcloud state, somewhat too expansively, that as much as one-third of the population of the United States is tattooed. Sooner or later, say the masters, this percentage will drift back to the shops to enlarge their skin-albums, to refresh the old lines, or to demand their surcharge or removal. For the sake of that inevitable custom, it behooves the masters to stick to their needles.

VI

the circus

1

THE idea of exhibiting white tattooed men for a fee was born among European visitors to the South Sea Islands and was first tried out in Western Europe. Joseph Cabri, a Frenchman tattooed while in the South Seas, returned to Europe where he was gravely studied by learned societies, exhibited to several crowned heads, and finally shown, in the most intimate detail, to any spectator who would pay the admission price. Thus he made a living for a number of years, but his skin shriveled with age, and in 1818 he died, obscure and poor, in Valenciennes, his birthplace. In 1843 Vincendon-Dumoulin and Desgraz described his life and adventures, voicing regret that his skin had not been preserved in alcohol to enlighten new generations. But other white men were returning to Europe from the Orient and the South Seas, with their skin tattooed, and the exhibition of these wonders was taken up by various entrepreneurs. From Europe the idea was brought over to America and exploited by the circus-owners.

Freaks are the important element in the "high romance and grotesque realism," the paradoxical *raison d'être* of the circus as defined by Joyce Kilmer. Freaks are the much needed escape from the humdrum. They are poetry. Poets are not freaks, but freaks are poets, said Kilmer. Like a poet, who puts his grief into fair words and shows it to the public in exchange for money and fame, so a circus freak displays his deformity to the awed gazers. "This poet," wrote Kilmer, "shows a soul scarred by the cruel whips of injustice; this man a back scarred by the tattooer's needles." Kilmer should have added that these tattooed backs are not only escape-poetry but also nightmarish dreams come true—atavistic dreams now possible of fruition. Here is the marking of the skin,—the way of our savage ancestors to win a woman, to frighten an enemy, to invoke magic. An American circus-goer, gazing at the tattooed man in the sideshow, relives his own past of untold centuries back. Moreover, he can now imitate the freak. He can get a tattooed design or two onto his own skin—and thus blissfully revert to his own distant, primitive type, incidentally experiencing a certain erotic pleasure in the process of being tattooed.

Thus the exhibition of tattooed freaks in the American circus was an early success. Dan Rice was among the first circus-managers to exploit the idea. In the years 1851 and 1852 he had among his players one James F. O'Connel. A tattooed man and a good drawing card was James F. O'Connel. But it remained for P. T. Barnum to pick the most famous example of a human picture gallery for his show and to exploit the public interest to the hilt. In the 1870's and 1880's Barnum boasted of his Georg (or Georgius) Constantine, whose skin presented the most complete, elaborate, and artistic tattooing ever witnessed in America or Europe. In the course of several years, during his incessant travels with Barnum's show through the length and breadth of America, the Burmese designs of this man left a more profound influence on the skin-puncturing art of this country than all the thousands of American Indian tattooers had been able to exert in the centuries before him.

Constantine was a Greek from Albania. His wild and dubious story was that in the middle 1860's he had participated in the French expedition to Cochin China. With a band of robbers he entered Bokhara or "Chinese Tartary" to commit depredations, or do some illegal gold-mining, but was taken prisoner by "the Chinese Tartars" in Burma. For ages Burma had been known as the classic country of tattooing. The human skin was ornamented by the Burmese sometimes as a religious rite or a charm against the weapons of enemies, sometimes for a fee, sometimes *pour l'art,* and quite often with special designs and writing as punishment to prisoners of war and to criminals. Constantine claimed he had received his ornaments as a cruel punishment lasting three months and administered by six tattooers. Three other prisoners, he said, had undergone the same operation together with him, but one of them had died at the hands of the tattooer, and another had gone stone blind. Later, Constantine (or the lecturer assigned him by Barnum) maintained that all three had died under the operation, and that he alone had survived the awful process. He also related that at the time of the operation his body was swollen enormously, and that ever since it had been extremely sensitive to weather changes.

At first glance it seemed to his observers that Constantine was covered from his hair to his toes by a close-fitting and transparent Turkish shawl. In Vienna a medical student, presumably none too keen-visioned, mistook him for a bronze statue. There was almost no part of his body, not a quarter-inch of the skin, free from designs. Even among his thick and curly hair some blue designs could be seen. Neither did his eyelids nor the interior of his ears remain untouched. Some observers claimed that the soles of his feet were spared by the tattooers, but an opposing school denies this fiercely. There were 388 designs on his body, arranged symmetrically and distributed thus: on his forehead 2 designs, on his neck and throat 8, breast 50, back 37, abdomen and buttocks 52, dorsum of penis 1, left arm 51, right arm 50, lower extremities 137. Here is, for instance, the catalogue of his breast, in part: two crowned sphinxes, two serpents, two swans, one horned owl. There were two dragons on his forehead. On his back, feet, and other parts of the body, an observer could see indigo and red monkeys, elephants, leopards, tigers, lions, panthers, gazelles, cats, crocodiles, lizards, eagles, storks, peacocks, fishes, men and women, salamanders, fruit, leaves and flowers, most of them quite small but exceptionally exact in their details. There were also lines of Oriental writing, especially in the interstices between his fingers. He said, proudly, that this writing branded him as "the greatest rascal and thief in the world."

When around 1870 Constantine came to Vienna, Professor Max Müller looked at the writing on the body and recognized it as Burmese. Constantine said that he could speak a half-dozen languages, and Professor Müller recognized fluent Arabic and Persian among them. Dr. J. Milner Fothergill, an Englishman, while in Vienna, examined Constantine and noted: "The tattooing is evidently done in the imitation of Doorga, the wife of Siva, the oldest demon god of India, and the red hands indicate her thirst for blood." There was no doubt that Constantine had been in the Orient for years, and that his tattooing was in the best Burmese style, but it was unlikely that he had acquired it as punishment or as a prisoner of war, for the Burmese writing, when translated by the experts, did not indicate this. The consensus of opinion among the scientists was that he had gone to Burma as a peaceful traveler and had paid some native master to be tattooed for purposes of exhibition.

The shrewd calculations of Constantine bore their pecuniary fruit. He was well paid in Vienna where Professor Ferdinand Hebra, the famous dermatologist, exhibited him to his students as the most remarkable and harmonious example of *ein tättowirter Mann,* or *Homo notis compunctus,* wrote about him in learned journals, and included a colored picture of his head and bust in his celebrated atlas. Among other things it was considered medically noteworthy that, despite his complete tattooing, Constantine's glands were not swollen and perspiration not affected; that in general, the forty-odd year old Greek was an almost lurid picture of health.

Barnum brought him to America, probably in 1873, amid the customary fanfares let loose at every discovery of his. He assigned a special lecturer to Constantine, and began to count quick profits for both himself and the wonder-man. It was said that he paid Constantine $1000 a week. Following his old custom of bestowing military titles upon his freaks, Barnum called his new find Captain Constantenus. Occasionally he was advertised as Prince Constantinus, the Turk, the Living Picture-Gallery. Today, in the American circus lingo this expression, "the picture-gallery," is firmly entrenched, applied to any tattooed man or woman.

The American circus-goers beheld in Constantine a rather large, well-built man taking graceful postures on a stand or a barrel. His head was hairy but in a way handsome. His clothing was, of course, scanty, consisting mostly of a loin-rag. When exhibited by Professor Hebra, the tattooed man wore his hair and beard naturally enough, but Barnum would not have this. Under his direction Constantine wore long braids, curled and fastened on the top of his head. On one of his fingers he had a huge solitaire diamond which be brought into play as he flourished a cigarette. In Boston a scientist had long talks with Constantine and felt his body here and there, vainly endeavoring to find a sign of deception. Con-

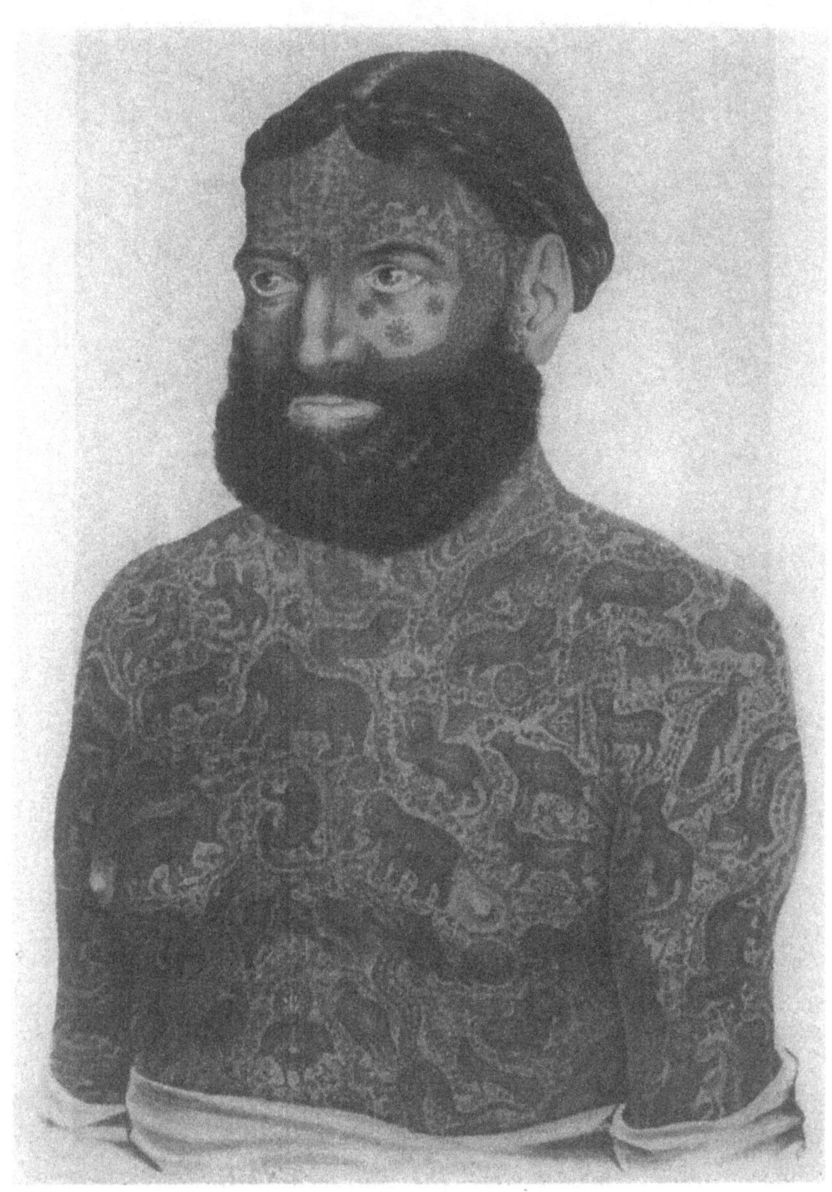

Constantine, top-section.

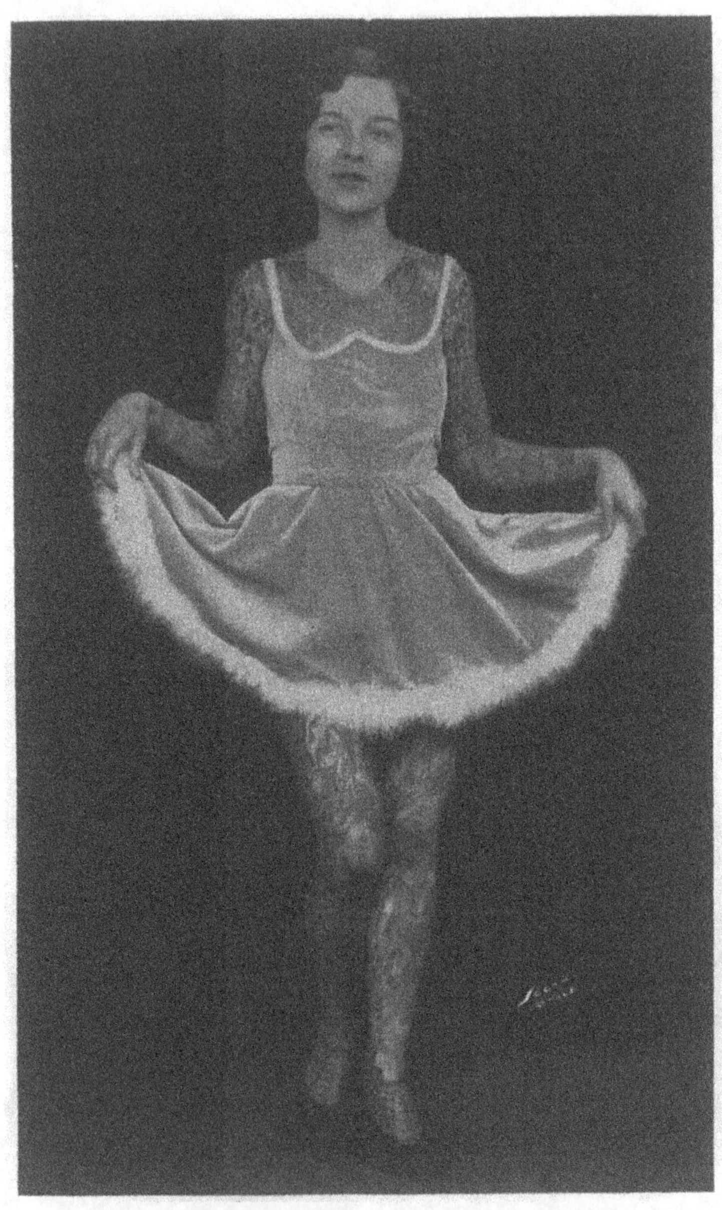

"Miss Stella," the Tattooed Lady
A highly attractive feminine exhibit, famous for her needlework.

stantine smiled proudly. Here was a happy extrovert whose exhibitionism was encouraged and rewarded. His wild stories, at which the learned men of Vienna sniffed so sceptically, were just what Barnum wanted. The stories were elaborated upon endlessly. Soon Constantine seemed to be the most desperate character ever to sign up with the great enterpriser.* His lecturer would wind up his spiel with the words: "And this wild tattooed man is always much admired by all the ladies." The erotic hint was a never failing smash and always brought down the house.

2

Professor Charlie Wagner tells me, dreamily, that he first saw Constantine in a Grand Street dime-museum sometime in the late 1880's. He was so deeply impressed with the spectacle that he got himself tattooed and began to learn in earnest the art of skin-incision. Since then, and to this day, Wagner has tattooed several hundreds of thousands of men and women in America, among them more than fifty celebrated performers for the American circus.

The influence of Constantine's tattoos was far reaching. The success of his exhibition prompted other circus-men to look for other tattooed exhibits—human canvas-backs. Men

* Nevertheless, Constantine was not the first white man covered by Burmese designs to come to this continent. In 1861, on his visit to Rivière du Loup, Canada, a certain Dr. Gascoigne met a man named Chambers, who after two days of friendly talk revealed that he had been tattooed many years back, while stationed in Burma as lieutenant of an English regiment. He stripped for the doctor, showing that he was tattooed from a collar round the neck to the wrists and to the middle of his calves, with the figures of Burmese gods and goddesses, also birds, beasts, fishes, scrolls and lines of Burmese writing. He said that he got tattooed "for the curiosity of the thing," paying forty pounds sterling to a native artist. In 1861, he was a tall, thin, gray-haired man, about fifty-two years old, poor and moody. He made a living by blowing a penny whistle and playing the concertina uncommonly well, but despite his poverty would not exhibit his body, for "he seemed ashamed of his youthful freak."

who already had some tattooed designs on their bodies now sought out masters to complete the skin-galleries and then proceeded to secure circus contracts. Salaries of one and two hundred dollars a week to tattooed big-time circus men were not infrequent.

Women and girls soon entered the profession, and from the very start proved a stronger attraction than most of the men, Constantine excepted. The American newspapers of the early 1880's treated as a sensation the reports about "a young woman in New York City who is undergoing the process of tattooing over nearly the whole body, avowedly to obtain a living by the exhibition." A few small-time, dime-museum women were reluctant to mar themselves for life, yet longed for the profits of a tattooed body. In 1896 W. L. Alden, in his book of semi-fiction, *Among the Freaks,** made one of his characters, a Chicago showman, say: "It was Barnum that invented the tattooed business, and for a while it was the best line of business in the profession. Every museum was bound to have a Tattooed Girl, with a yarn about her having been captured by the Indians and tattooed when she was a little girl." The man then explained that in his show, as in some others, "the tattooing is put on every Monday with a stencil plate and brush, and is generally washed off on Saturday night when it begins to get faded." The point of the story comes when, to avenge a jilted lover of Jemima, the "tattooed" girl, wrong plates are used on her back and arms, and she comes out on the platform, tattooed with such sentiments as Keep Dry, Very Fragile, Handle With Care, Strictly Private, and This Side Up.

Soon some of the American Indians performing in the Wild West shows began to feel that if anyone should exploit skin-ornaments it was the originators of tattooing on this continent. In the 1880's and 1890's, more and more tattooed

* New York: Longmans, Green and Co.

Indians appeared with the traveling shows. There were women among them, too. At the turn of the century, at Austin and Stone's Museum in Boston, an American white juggler and his American Indian wife performed with much success. Her whole body, including legs and arms, was covered with many genuine tattoo designs which she said were the best North American Indian work ever achieved, but in reality were nothing but good work of the American white tattoo-masters. By this time it was not enough for a tattooed man or woman to sit or stand idly and draw the stares of admission-payers. A tattooed performer had to perform. This Indian woman joined her husband in executing various juggling tricks. She also called herself an Indian prophetess and did some mind-reading. Undoubtedly, in the eyes of her clients, her tattooings enhanced her purported magic powers. The American success of this couple led to trips abroad, where both learned to speak German and French.

Of the American white women in the tattooed ranks, May Brooks and Annie Howard were well known, playing circuses in the summer and dime-museums in the winter. Annie Howard, together with her brother Frank, was with Barnum and Bailey's show in the early 1900's. Annie and Frank's story was that they were born in Pennsylvania, shipwrecked in the Pacific Ocean and rescued by savages who tattooed them until every inch of their bodies, except their faces, hands, and feet, was covered by wondrous scenes and figures. Charlie Wagner confirms my suspicions by telling me that Frank Howard was tattooed not by any savages but by such God-fearing Americans as Hildebrandt and Steve Lee; that Annie Howard was tattooed by O'Reilly and "finished off" by her brother. Frank Howard continued on the circus wheel for many years. Having learned the puncturing art, he quit the circus to open a tattoo-shop in Boston (Court Street), in partnership with Ed Smith, an O'Reilly disciple. It was one of the biggest tattoo-shops on the east coast of America. Frank died some time about 1920, and Ed Smith some ten years later.

In the interval between Constantine and the Howards, Barnum's show had John Hayes. Hayes used to say that he was born in Ansonia, Connecticut, in 1864, and that at the age of fourteen he joined the American army as a drummer boy. His regiment was sent to fight the Indians in the Far West, and in one of the battles young John became separated from his fellow-soldiers and was captured by the Apache braves. He said that among the Redmen he found a white man, a former sailor who had married an Indian squaw. It was this sailor, said Hayes, who placed 780 tattoo designs on his body, from his neck to his heels, the operation taking 154 days. But again Charlie Wagner bobs up with the information that Professor O'Reilly did most of the work on John's body, though it was possible that the first few designs had been executed by someone else.*

The circus people liked O'Reilly's newfangled electric machine. They considered its work clearer and more artistic than the result of the old hand method. It was not therefore surprising that most of the circus tattoo-celebrities came to him for improvement on the old designs, for additions to their galleries, or for the creation of a gallery where there was none before. In addition to Hayes, he tattooed such mainstays of the circus as Mr. and Mrs. Williams, Frank De Burgh and his wife Emma, Calavan and Mellivan. The Williamses and the De Burghs went to England where they were exhibited, each couple separately, for many years and with much success. Calavan was one of the first ones to tattoo those American circus-patrons who came to gasp at

* The experiences of a drummer-boy, including the intimate acquaintance with the white sailor who married a squaw, were at one time claimed also by Frank Howard as his very own.

him. He made and saved a lot of money, and now owns a hotel in Philadelphia. George Mellivan was the first native American tattooed man to reach a $200-a-week salary mark, but he lived to see and lament the day when some circus-owners, aware of profits like those of Calavan's, not only avoided paying salaries to the tattooed men and women but treated their presence in the circus as a concession and made the tattooed performers pay for it. Thus Mellivan, starting in the big-time at a salary of $200 a week, ended by paying to get into the circus. He died a true trooper, while traveling with his show, somewhere in the South.

The small-time wages to the tattooed people began to slide down about thirty years ago. Among the tattooers the popular legend is that the slide began when a New York dime-museum made the error of advertising a "Congress of Tattooed Men." This had the effect of convincing the public that, since there was a congress of them, such freaks could be rare no longer. The box-office receipts began to decrease, and so did salaries. From $60 a week for a tattooed male, the dime-museum scale diminished to $30 a week for a tattooed couple. But competition had been growing ferocious long before the Congress. As early as the 1880's, to outstrip the rivals, New York's dime-museums had whole Tattooed Families on exhibit. One family even had a tattooed Great Dane on the platform. Captain Burt Thompson tried to follow suit and tattooed his pet dog for a Coney Island show, but a fond spectator stole the animal. At about the same time, in the same Coney Island, another entrepreneur showed a tattooed cow.

In the middle 1880's, Barnum exhibited tattooed dwarfs. Immediately, there appeared tattooed wrestlers, tattooed knife-throwers, a tattooed Fat Lady or two. Lately there was an American daredevil motorcycle rider, tattooed all over.

who, by way of Manila, came to perform in Tokyo and other Far Eastern points.

3

The phenomenon of tattooed circus women was vastly intriguing to the crowd. In due time the American and British masses responded by singing a freshly created folksong, to the tune of *My Home in Tennessee,* but known under its own title, *The Tattooed Lady.* It seemed to have originated in England, but the North American devotees of the song never failed to insert special American and Canadian words and phrases into the text. Of course, it was not about *any* tattooed lady, but most particularly about a *circus* tattooed lady:

I paid a bob to see
The tattooed Scotch lady
Tattooed from head to knee
She was a sight to see.
For over her jaw
Was a British man-o'-war,
While on her back
Was the Union Jack,
And could one ask for more?
All up and down her spine
Was the King's horse guard in line,
And all about her hips
Was a line of battleships,
And over one kidney
Was a bird's-eye view of Sidney,
But what I liked best,
Across her chest
Was my home in Tennessee.

In John Dos Passos' *1919* this tattooed lady becomes French. The song was as much of a success as the lady it described. It was particularly popular during the World War; in the trenches, to which it was brought allegedly by the Australians, but where it was shouted by all the English-speaking troops: the Anzacs, the Tommies. the Canadians, the South Africans, and the Yanks.

The tattooed man of the sideshow also found his way into the American song. The most famous composition ran as follows:

Do you remember, Angeline,
That heartless "Human Snake"?
Who won my heart, in another part,
And gave that heart a break?
I'll sing you now of my sweet revenge,
'Twas retribution stern;
She fell in love with a tattooed man,
Who broke her heart in turn.

CHORUS:

He was such a human picture gallery,
Such a spectacular gent;
He won her heart and drew her salary,
He never gave a cent.
Till one good day, with her season's pay
And the Fat Lady off he ran,
Oh, 'tis perfectly true, you can beat a tattoo,
But you can't beat a tattooed man.

He had designs upon himself,
She had designs on him;
She loved to look at the picture book
He had on every limb;

"Oh why should I go abroad?" she said,
"To Germany, France or Rome,
With a lovely collection awaiting inspection
In my happy little home?"

CHORUS:

He'd Raphael's Cherubs on his brow,
The Angelus on his chest;
While on his back, was a liberal stack
Of Old Masters of the best.
"Oh, picture to yourself," she said,
"A lovelorn maiden's doom."
"I cannot picture to myself," he said,
*"For there's no more room."**

But the most surprising imprint left by Barnum's importation revealed itself in the field of American national politics. It has been said, and not with exaggeration, that the Tattooed Man of the circus influenced the result of the presidential campaign of 1884, robbing James G. Blaine of his White House chance, and helping Grover Cleveland to the laurels of his first term.

The man who introduced the figure of the tattooed Greek into American politics was a young Englishman, Bernard Gillam, an artist with *Puck*, an independent Republican weekly with strong anti-Blaine inclinations. Gillam conceived the idea of representing the presidential aspirants as the inmates of a freak sideshow. In *Puck's* issue of April 16, this

* It was performed by Frank Daniels, a popular comic opera actor of the 1890's. The song was part of *The Idol's Eye*, dialogue and lyrics by Harry B. Smith, music by Victor Herbert, first produced at the Broadway Theatre, New York, on October 25, 1897, and thenceforth repeated for many months and years with a great success. In 1931, Joseph Kaye, the biographer of Victor Herbert, remarked: "The human picture gallery idea has been used in various forms since *The Idol's Eye*. The last transformation can be seen today as a burlesque stock bit, in which the anatomical illustrations are not quite so aesthetic as Smith made them."

cartoon appeared with Blaîne filling the fancy skin and flimsy tights of the Tattooed Man, occupying a prominent place in the foreground.

Gillam made even Blaine's beard resemble the Greek's hirsute ornaments, and there were the Greek's earrings. Yet Blaine as Blaine was recognizable enough. As Constantine boasted of his depredations, so Blaine's body was shown inscribed with the scandals charged against him by his enemies. The "tattooed" inscriptions on Blaine's body read: Bribery, Bluster, Guano Statesmanship, Mulligan Letters, N. Pacific Bonds, Anti-Chinese Demagogism.*

The cartoon created an unprecedented furor, and the figure of the "tattooed" Blaine was held as the chief, if not the only, reason. The issue of April 16 sold a quarter of a million extra copies. The success had to be followed up. From then on, and until the close of the campaign, a number of Gillam's cartoons appeared in *Puck* picturing Blaine in sundry difficulties and amid different personages, but almost invariably it was as the Tattooed Man that he appeared and was made to speak his lines. One of these cartoons showed Blaine looking into the water of a lily pond and admiring his "tattooed" reflection Narcissus-like. In this particular instance Gillam perhaps unconsciously seized upon one of the chief inherent reasons for tattooing—its narcissist base.

The National Democratic Committee ordered *Puck* in huge stacks whenever the Tattooed Man graced its pages, and distributed it as excellent campaign-literature. The catchy two words were presently picked up by other pro-Cleveland periodicals. These periodicals heralded Blaine's stumping tour around the country under such headings as:

* Gillam was not quite original. Back in 1876 the German edition of *Puck* used a cartoon by Joseph Keppler showing a tattooed figure of Columbia, shamed by such inscriptions on her fair body as Whisky Ring, Tammany, Election Frauds, Corruption, Taxes, Black Friday, Secession, Credit Mobilier, and Taxes.

"Tattooed Man Arrives." The New York *Times* ran the account of the grand dinner given at Delmonico's by Jay Gould and some of his associates to Blaine, under the heading:

FEEDING THEIR CANDIDATE

THE MONOPOLISTS' DINNER TO THE TATTOOED MAN

The streets, too, rang with the singular expression. The Clevelandites paraded, swaying their lighted torches, and jeering:

Jim! Jim! Tat-tooed Jim!
Jim! Jim! Tat-tooed Jim!

In years to come, Cleveland readily acknowledged his debt to Gillam's creation and *Puck's* editorials, saying that the Tattooed Man quips and thunders had done more than any other single influence used in the campaign to elect him. The force of the idea told not only on the result of the close election contest but on the serenity of Blaine himself. He was incensed, particularly by the word "Bribery" gracing his skin in the cartoons, and at length wanted to bring a suit against the publishers of *Puck*. It took the strongest pressure of his friends to stop him.

The anti-climax of the story lies in the fact that throughout the campaign Gillam himself remained a regular Republican. The sense of guilt, so often manifested by a tattooer toward his client after the job is done, was manifested by Gillam. He felt almost as if Blaine were raped by him. After each cartoon of Blaine, the Tattooed Man, was printed in *Puck*, Gillam would, more or less secretly, suggest an anti-Cleveland cartoon to the artists of *Judge*. On Election Day he voted for Blaine.

the circus

4

Naturally, the circus is not the only place where tattoo-exhibitionism is tied up with the profit motive. Tattooing had been tried in America as a straight advertising medium. "I once undertook," reminisced the late Frank Howard, "to tattoo a man for a popular cigar store—he was to be a living panorama of pictures of the store in question, to be shown at the fairs." Wagner recalls a tattoo-ad of a drive-yourself-garage he did on the back of a bathing-beach frequenter. In certain American seaport-cities many business men think it good business policy to have tattooed marks on their hands or wrists where they can be readily seen by sailors and other customers. The latest touch was provided by one K. Marampus, the owner of a suit and dress repairing shop in New York, who last August ordered from Al Neville the tattoo of a Blue Eagle for his chest, with that dramatic prosperity-restoring inscription: N. R. A.—We Do Our Part. He says he bares his chest before every customer. But the circus and dime-museum remain the main objectives of those who wish to exploit their tattoos for monetary returns.

At the present writing, there are about three hundred completely tattooed men and women in this country, making, or trying to make, a living by exhibiting themselves. The modern annals of tattooed people exhibiting in America are mainly the story of woman's predominance. The circus managers found that tattooed girls mean a better box-office than tattooed men. They also found out from practical experience that the younger and the prettier these girls are the healthier the receipts.

The workings of the mind of a young modern American girl, before she decides to have her body tattooed for the purposes of commercial exhibition, are admirably illustrated by the following letter received by Mrs. Stevens, the Fat Lady tattooed by Frank Graf:

Buffalo, N. Y., Oct. 17, 1932.

Dear Mrs. Stevens:—

Your name and address were furnished to me by Mr. F. G. Graf, tattoo artist, who has done work for a gentleman friend of mine, and whom I am considering to tattoo me for exhibition in circuses etc.

Before deciding finally, however, I wanted to talk with or hear from some lady who had been covered as to whether she would advise me to have myself covered. I have a butterfly on my arm and so I know about the hurting and that part of it but am wondering if I would be apt to be sorry right away about having it done. Some of my girl friends think I will be. Were you sorry, Mrs. Stevens? Also please tell me whether you found it difficult to let people look at you when you were on exhibition or do you soon get used to it.

I am a stenographer but am not working. It isn't the right work for me, anyway, as I am not the kind to be tied down to a job of that kind but would like to travel around and I like excitement. I am twenty-three years old and five ft. two inches tall and weigh 112 lbs. My figure is good I think. I swim a lot. Do you think, if I had nice tattooing on me, I would be able to find work all right. I saw a girl with Ringling Bros. circus a year ago last summer—not a large girl—and she was beautifully covered. That was when I started thinking about it.

I hate to bother you, a perfect stranger to me, Mrs. Stevens, but don't know anyone else to ask about these things. Please write to me as soon as you can and tell me what you think of the idea. I want to get started soon if I'm going to do it. I would like you to tell me something about what tattooed girls earn, too.

I am not married—not much interested in men. The friend I spoke about is partly covered and when I see him in a bathing suit I can hardly wait to get started, too, and then again sometimes I grow rather doubtful.

Anything you may see fit to write me about your own feelings after you get tattooed will be very much appreciated, Mrs. Stevens.

Again apologizing for the nuisance this will mean to you, I am

Very truly yours,

EDNA V.

After they acquire tattoos and mount the platform, they recall or invent the most romantic stories as to the origin of their tattoos, they appeal for pity, they denounce those who had caused them to be disfigured for life. Yet at the same time they relish the memory of the betrayal and the operation. In 1925 Victoria James, a dime-museum tattooed girl of New York, said to a tabloid sob-sister:

> I was tattooed for love and live to regret it. Heaven may forgive the man who so swayed my youthful heart as to cause me to submit to his fiendish treatment, but I cannot. I have tried to forgive him, but every time I look upon my mutilated skin, from neck to toes, my heart rebels and I cannot help but hate him. . . . John had no mercy. He cut and cut, and filled the crevices with ink until my very veins were clogged with it. . . . I am an attraction today—Pictoria, the Tattooed Lady, they call me, the creature whose white body has been turned into inky blue designs. Day by day the crowds come to look at me—to examine my seared flesh. Little do they know what the exhibition costs in human suffering—or that a foolish girl submitted to it out of love for a human fiend with a pair of flashing eyes.

Thus the exhibition of tattooed women in the American sideshow becomes heavily and frankly tinged with the sex motive. The story of a sex betrayal is always here, and it matters little whether it is actual or imaginary. Now not the coarse hoydens of yore, but dainty females are recruited for the platform. Thus we see Betty Broadbent, an artist's model, quitting Greenwich Village to undergo the tattooing operation in hopes of a circus fortune. This she has achieved, and more: she got into vaudeville, reached Hollywood, hobnobbed with Tom Mix and other film stars. No less beautiful and chic is Mae Vandermark of the Ringling circus. A native of Pennsylvania, Mae came to New York in 1924 to work as a stenographer, and in a short time secured a position in the Plaza Hotel. One day, while swimming in Coney Island, she saw a butterfly tattooed on a girl's shoulder. She liked it so well that forthwith she sought out a boardwalk tattooer and ordered two butterflies for herself, one on each shoulder. Then she met Miss Pictoria (Victoria James), who easily persuaded Mae to become a professional tattooed woman. She took Mae to Wagner who covered her. She started to play in a Coney Island show, adopting Miss Artorio as her new name, and then graduating into the big-time.

While on tour with a circus in the summer of 1927 the India Rubber Man fell in love with her. Professor Henri, in real life Clarence H. Alexander of Ypsilanti, Michigan, could stretch his neck seven inches, his arms and legs twelve inches. He was forty-three years old, a professional freak since he was twenty-three. She was twenty, a trooper less than two years. Their associates called them "Tattooed Mae and Rubber November," sadly noting that Mae lacked a trooper's psychology. She was a spectator, the Rubber Man was to her not a fellow-player and a possible life-mate, but a freak. While Henri Alexander was in love with her tattooings she was repelled by his deformity. She was frightened when he used his elastic magic to pass love notes to her over the heads of the Fat Lady and the Midget sitting between them on the platform.

The love-smitten Rubber Man was moved away from the Tattooed Lady. It was thought that since it was her tattooing he was in love with, and since from now on he would not see her except in her street clothes, his love would surely die. But no. He pined for her and her tattooing, and finally took strychnine while on the circus platform. He collapsed and died a few minutes later.

With the advent of young and beautiful girls into the ranks of the circus tattooed people, and with the spread of their exhibition to vaudeville, the designs on the bodies underwent a quite marked change. Up till lately patriotic designs such as eagles, flags, and Statues of Liberty predominated on the bodies of the circus men and women. Large religious pieces were next in popularity: the Lord's Prayer, Madonna and Child, the reproduction of Leonardo da Vinci's Last Supper, Christ's head in a crown of thorns. Most of the religious designs were placed either on the upper part of the back or on the chest, which sections of the body had been, by the way, the favorite areas to be scourged by primitive flagellants. With the showmen it was not piety that moved them, but rather a sense of guilt, however vague and unconscious. Religious designs represented their attempt to convince themselves and the spectators that tattooing was not a thing of ugliness or shame or desecration. Frequently there was a message above or beneath a religious design, such as the Golden Rule, or "Love One Another," or "Jesus Saves." This attached a missionary element to the fact of tattooing and to the act of its exhibition. Thus sin was absolved. Then there were daggers with inscriptions: "Death Before Dishonor," also bleeding hearts, and naked females of crudely sensuous aspects. These, as well as the patriotic and religious designs, were known in the profession as "American work." English tattoo-masters, such as Sutherland Macdonald of London, maintained that the American work was influenced by the old tattoo-designs of the sailors' fancy. The Oriental animals, birds, and insects were in but secondary favor as far as the American circus tattoo people were concerned. But with young and pretty girls coming into the profession the daintier Japanese and Burmese art is returning, with its motifs of dragons, butterflies, geisha girls, flowers, defined by the proud tattooers as "high-class groteskew."

These attractive maidens also practise the active side of the tattoo art and decorate, for a fee, any of the spectators who hanker for skin-gravures. Girls and women give their custom to these women-masters. It is a long cry from the wild and terrifying Burmese designs of Barnum's hairy Greek, but it is his heritage nevertheless.

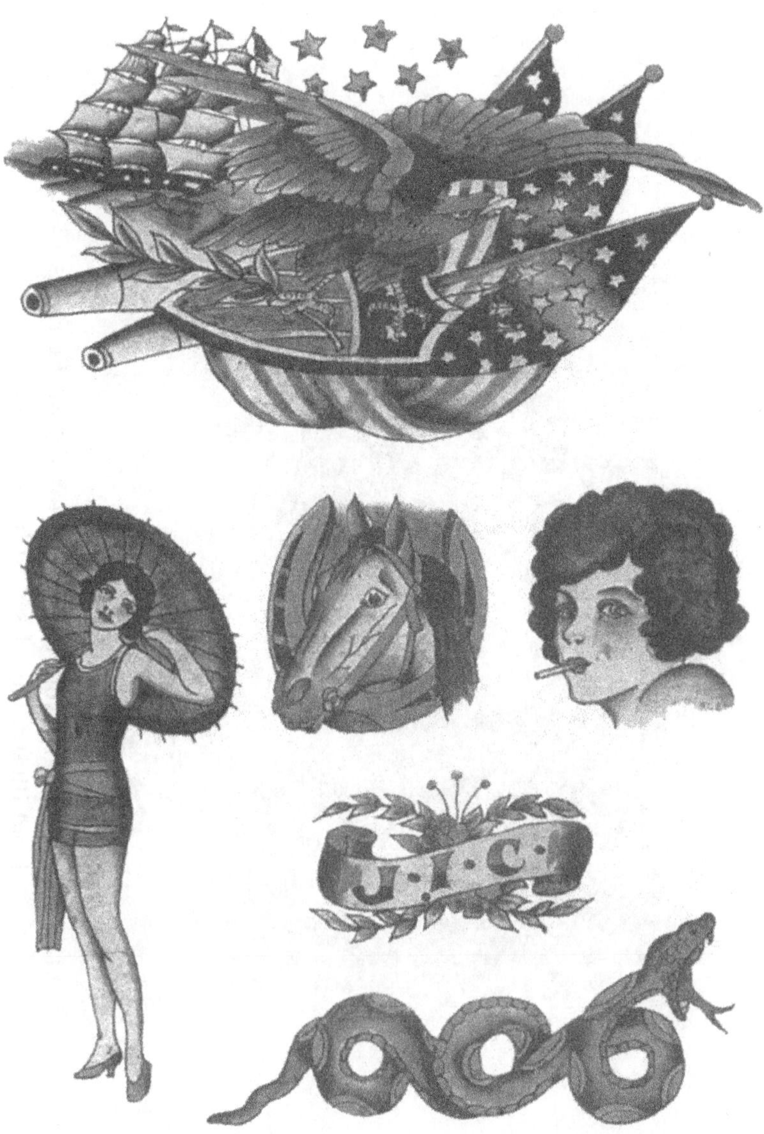

Some typical patterns popular with sailors. The horseshoe and snake symbols are, of course, rooted in familiar superstitions.

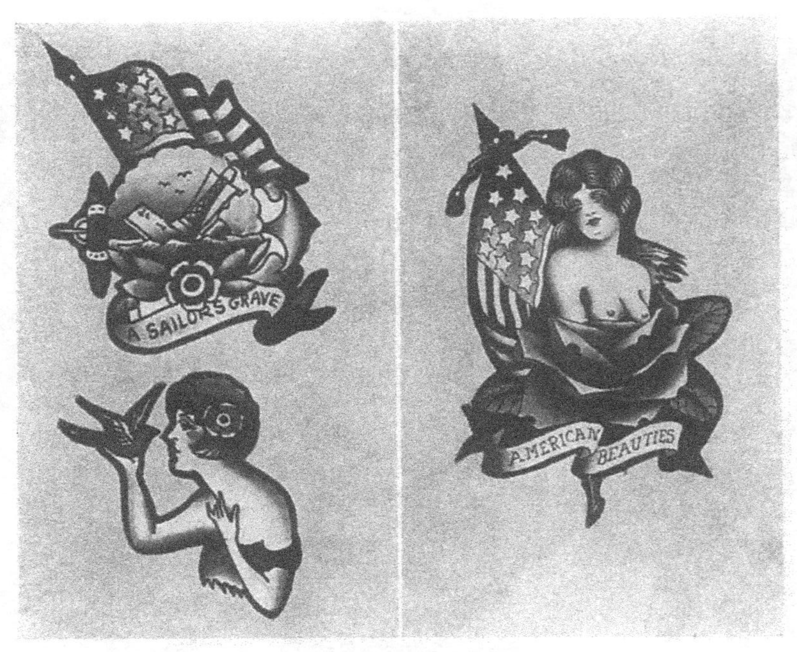

More sailors' tattoos. Note the happy linking, in the right-hand illustration, of sex with patriotism.

VII

sailors

1

Electric Elmer used to say: "Some of the men I turn out are as proud as a turkey with two tails. They'd like to go around with their coats off in the winter time just to show my clever work."

Exhibitionism plays a tremendous role in tattooing. Not always is it exploited for material gain. Outside the commercial sideshow tattoo-exhibitionism is most often encountered among sailors, those bold extroverts. It is among the sailors that the forearms are tattooed more frequently than other parts of the body. It is not only because the designs are subconsciously thought to give strength to these important members, but also because the forearms are more easily exposed at their owner's will. They are the best venue of his exhibitionism. There have been cases where sailors who carried on their chests the words and music of such songs as "Home Sweet Home" or "Where Is My Wandering Boy Tonight?" stripped in convivial company and had the songs performed for them, ostensibly for the sentiment of the thing, but in fact because it gave them an ingenious opportunity to draw attention to themselves.

Some men acquire tattoos to impress the beholders with the glamor of their adventures in far-off lands. Tattoo stands for exotic shores and the exhibitor's intimate acquaintance with their romance. Sailors often say that they get tattooed "to show the folks back home."* Charles L. Richards, of Chicago, writes to me: "Did you know that certain devices adorning sailors' bodies used to have a special significance and were a 'rate' the observance of which was rigidly adhered to? An anchor signified that the wearer had made a cruise on the Atlantic Ocean, a full-rigged ship that the sailor had sailed around Cape Horn, and a dragon that the wearer had actually been on the China station."

It is respect more than sympathy or fear or envy that the tattooed exhibit of the sideshow, or non-circus exhibitionist, hopefully expects. Similarly, a tattooed sailor wants to be respected for the "heroism," with which he endured the pain of tattooing. All tattoo marks are to him symbols of fearlessness and toughness, but certain themes may be selected for special emphasis. Thus many American sailors and marines have on their chests extensive reproductions of battles in Cuba, the Philippines or France in which they took part. Here we note the connection, however indirect, with the American Indians who used to get tattooed with pictorial representations of their heroic exploits in battles and hunts.

To indulge in tattooing, sailors had better opportunities than other extroverts of other strata of society. In Chapter II on *Men and Love* I quoted a London writer who back in 1881 compared tattooing to Yankee whittling, ascribing both to the same causes of "brainless indolence" and subconscious sadism. The forced idleness, whether brainy or brainless, while sails hung still in windless weather, was responsible for

* Similarly, in the fall of 1931, the London *Morning Post* reported that some American tourists ordered from English tattooers views of London "to take home as a tattooed souvenir."

the ships' wooden figureheads and other ingenious carvings as well as for tattoos on the sailors' bodies. An unnamed old sailor of the Seamen's Institute in New York, recalling those old days, inadvertently stressed the homosexual explanation of the sailors' tattooing:

> In the old days every man of the sea was tattooed, even the captain. That's the way they entertained themselves on board ship. The boys used to prick the marks in their skin and fill them with ink. Some of them had regular tattooing sets. There was plenty of time in those days. . . . The old sailor was an ignorant fellow. Think what it meant to go for months without hearing a thing that was happening in the world. All that time, too, he would not see a woman except, maybe, the captain's wife. No wonder he was a bashful fellow, ill at ease with ladies. (The New York *Times,* September 28, 1924.)

Doctor Bromberg confirms, in his observations:

> In the days when being a sailor was a profession, self-tattooing by shipmates was quite common. The whole atmosphere of the ship is conducive to bringing to the fore the homosexual drives that are unexpressed or sublimated in many persons. The very freedom of varied sexual experiences, the absence of binding home and sex ties attracts the types that have predominating homosexual components.

Because of this homosexual atmosphere, and of this idleness on long voyages, also because of their early opportunities to visit the Orient with its tattooed natives, the American sailors (as well as the sailors of all other Western nations) became known for their love of body-ornamentation. Professor O'Reilly used to declare solemnly that an American sailor without a tattoo was like a ship without grog—not seaworthy, (a bit of clever propaganda which, incidentally, tended to make tattooing among sailors an obligatory initiation ceremonial). Early in this century a legend was current among the American marines that a pious millionairess had once offered fifty dollars to any marine who had served two terms of enlistment without being tattooed, and not one yet had been able to claim the prize.* Miss Eleanor Barns, of the Seamen's Institute, once remarked: "A sailor may not wear his heart upon his sleeve, but he does wear it upon his chest, across the broad-muscled expanse of his back or upon the brawny bulge of his biceps. Some people pour out their colorful stories to juries. Others relieve the tension by writing for the confession magazines. The sailor enlists the tattooer's needle and upon his own body in dull blues, vivid reds, greens and yellows records the story of his loves and hates, his triumphs, his religion, and his patriotism."

The sailor's love-tattooings as well as his body-designs of faith and magic are described at length elsewhere in this book, in the chapters devoted to these particular motives. Love, faith and magic patterns are not peculiar to him, but patriotism tattoos are. He had sailed the seas when the American republic was young and weak, at best an upstart among the great powers. Thrown constantly amid strangers, the American sailor carried his patriotic tattoos as a chip on his shoulder. He proclaimed the grand qualities of the newly-born United States by the black and red Columbias, flags, portraits of George Washington, and proud mottoes on his arms and chest. It was the old striving to frighten the enemy with magic representations of the tribe's invincibility.

Patriotic themes gained in popularity greatly with the Civil

* This legend was first recorded by A. T. Sinclair in 1908 in the *American Anthropologist*. In 1933 I heard the following version of this legend, from a sailor patient in Beekman Street Hospital in New York: "The prize was offered by the Vanderbilts because they got tired of hearing that one of their women married a tattooed sailorman. They figure that the prize will prove that they are against tattooing." See Chapter VIII, page 105.

War. Some sailors carried on their chests or backs elaborate reproductions of such glorious battles as between the *Monitor* and the *Merrimac*, or the *Alabama* and the *Kearsarge*. Imitative soldiers and civilians, too, went in for flags, eagles, Uncle Sams, and Columbias. Stephen Vincent Benét in his *John Brown's Body* notes the case of a pathetic Jezebel who had herself tattooed with a Secesh flag: "She cried so hard when the Union troops were landed that the madam had to hide her down in the cellar." The Spanish-American War was another boon to the patriotic elements in the tattooers' business. One day O'Reilly counted 130 naval reservists in his studio. After the conflict he issued a pamphlet extolling his sailor-customers and linking tattoo with their love for their country:

> The glory of a man-o'-wars man at Santiago and elsewhere was to be stripped to the waist, his trousers rolled up to his knees, his white skin profusely decorated in tattoo; begrimed with powder, they were the men to do or die. Brave fellows! Little fear had they of shot and shell, amid the smoke of battle and after the scrub down they gloried in their tattoos.

So much ardor was put by the masters into these patriotic tattooings that even foreigners were charmed into ordering American emblems. Al Neville, the Welshman, showed me his chest decorated by a Hindoo tattooist, in hand fashion, combining an American eagle and an American flag with a Union Jack centerpiece. It dates to the times preceding at least by a decade the Anglo-American alliance of 1917-1918. Among the French sailors examined and reported by Lacassagne* there was one whose back was adorned with a large

* Dr. Alexandre Lacassagne (1843-1924) was a French army surgeon and the professor of medical jurisprudence of the Faculty of Medicine at Lyons. In the late 1870's, while in Algeria, he examined, for their tattooings, several hundred soldiers and navy men who had been condemned for desertion, insubordination, thefts, and other offenses and, on expiration of their prison

American Indian holding an American flag. He said that he had ordered it while in New York from an Irishman, "who was much reputed amongst the sailors, both for the excellence of his work and for the rapidity with which he did it." The Irishman must have been no other than O'Reilly. It was also he who fostered among sailors and longshoremen such variations of patriotic expression as the American and Irish flags intertwined, with "Erin Go Bragh" and "Hands Across the Sea" etched beneath. Thus patriotism gradually softened into internationalism, reaching its apogee in the "Flags of All Nations" design.

2

In 1908 A. T. Sinclair wrote that of the American man-of-war's men fully ninety percent were tattooed, and that the same was true of the American deep-water sailors, also of the coasters and the marines. The same percentage, said Sinclair, applied to the Scandinavian deep-water men, among whom the tradition was said to be very ancient. However, among the American fishermen sailing in 1908 from Boston, Cape Cod and vicinity, only about ten percent bore tattooed devices. I would explain this low percentage by the puritanic feelings against tattooing then still strong with the native-stock men of New England. It was characteristic that, according to Sinclair, those of the local fishermen who had marks on their bodies had acquired them while on foreign voyages or on trips down the American coast to the relatively non-puritanic ports.

At about the same time Sinclair interviewed some two hundred Italian fishermen in Boston, mostly Sicilians hailing

sentences, sent to *les bataillons d'Afrique* to finish the remainder of their military service. He copied 1,333 tattoo-designs from the bodies of 378 soldier- and sailor-offenders, and published the result of his studies in a volume entitled, *Les tatouages, étude anthropologique et médico-légale,* (Paris, 1881).

from Messina, Palermo and Catania, and found not a single tattoo among them. George Tichenor, a writer and ex-sailor, tells me that in the American merchant marine men of Scandinavian descent are the most tattooed, because the designs stand out clearly on their fair skin, while the Italian-descent men are tattooed the least because of their darker skin.*

In 1913 Surgeon A. Farenholt of the United States Navy made public the result of a series of investigations conducted by him over a period of more than twelve years. He estimated that, generally speaking, about sixty percent of the men in the naval service, who have been in the navy ten or more years, bear upon their skin one or more tattooed designs. In examining the records of 3,575 men who were enlisted on the receiving ship *Independence* at San Francisco during a period of eight and a half years, Dr. Farenholt found that fifty percent of the men coming for their second enlistment bore tattooing, and that the percentage of tattooed men among the applicants for their first enlistment did not exceed twenty-three. More than half of those tattooed had acquired their skin-pictures after they entered the navy. An average marine, even though he had served nearly as much time at sea as an average bluejacket, was not so prone to get tattooed, perhaps because the marine "never feels himself to be purely a seafaring man." Dr. Farenholt believed the Oriental in-

* However, the New York *Evening World,* of July 10, 1915, reported that many Italian reservists returning from New York to Italy to serve in the army acquired some tattoos before they sailed. It is well known that Sicilians predominate in the Italian colony of New York. Similarly, my own observations show that at the present time most of the Bowery's tattoo-clients are youths of Italian (Sicilian) parentage. The skin of these is perhaps lighter than that of their parents or grandparents because of the different climatic conditions under which they grew up. The dark skin argument would apply to American Negroes rather than to American Italians. There are very few tattooed Negroes in this country, and the reason is not their fear of pain, as Harry Lawson tried to tell me. Among the few cases of Negroes with tattoos on their skin known to me there is the proprietress of a Negro newspaper in a large Atlantic coast city (a heart on her arm), but she is so light of color that she could easily pass for white.

fluence to be a decisive factor in the tattooing of an average American bluejacket, not so much in the nature of the designs selected as in the very incentive to acquire bodily decorations: "In the Orient he finds more tattooed men than he ever saw at home, and he also finds more people ready to lend their art to his adornment if the price is forthcoming."

Dr. Farenholt found the forearm the first place to be tattooed, the arms next, the chest third, the shoulders fourth, the hands fifth. Then, in order of their preference, came the wrists, the legs, the feet, the back, and finally the face. Thus the motive of exhibitionism is confirmed as the strongest among the sailors. They prefer to have those parts of the body tattooed which can be easily exposed to the outsiders' view, yet as easily withdrawn from the hostile or mocking gaze. This explains why the forearm is most frequently tattooed, the face most rarely.

In ancient times not infrequently slaves and criminals were branded or tattooed on the face. The legend had it that Cain's mark was on his face. In *Omoo* Herman Melville wrote that Lem Hardy's tattoo of a shark on the forehead was "far worse than Cain's." Hardy was an Englishman gone native on a South Sea island. Melville and his fellow-sailors "gazed upon this man with a feeling akin to horror, no ways abated when informed that he had voluntarily submitted to this embellishment of his countenance." Years later, lecturing in Boston, Melville revealed that he too had been in danger of acquiring tattoos on the face from his insistent South Sea hosts, but had successfully combated all their attempts, for which escape he fervently thanked God.

There is, however, a legend current among American sailormen that some of the crew of the *Kearsarge* immediately after the Civil War formed the so-called Star Gang by ordering the tattoo of a star on their forehead, in commemoration of their heroism in the battle with the *Alabama*. They perhaps felt that for heroism as great as theirs the use of the forehead was excusable; that this extreme form of exhibitionism was no more than warranted by the bright glory of their ship.*

Symbols and inscriptions in memory of certain extraordinary events were not infrequent among the tattoos of the American sailors. Even in our modern days they are still being ordered by the devotees. Recently a submarine sailor ordered upon his broad back this tattoo inscription, in a border of doves, wreaths and ocean waves: ONLY SURVIVOR OF THE S-4; MAY MY COMRADES REST IN PEACE. The tribute to the lost comrades was merely a polite afterthought, the more important fact was that he was the only survivor. His pride was not diminished by the detail that he was a hero by reflection only: he was not in the catastrophe, as two days before he had broken his leg and been transferred from the ill-fated submarine to another ship.

According to Dr. Farenholt, all sorts of lettering, including lucky numbers, important dates, happy mottoes, and wordy tributes to lost comrades or past glories, held first place in the navymen's favor; then, in order of their popularity, came coats of arms, flags, anchors, eagles and other birds, stars, female figures, ships, clasped hands, daggers, crosses, bracelets, and hearts. The occupational sea-symbols, such as Neptunes, mermaids and fishes he found in steadily diminishing numbers, while such "dude" pictures as those of tennis rackets, bats and balls, etc., he discovered with increasing frequency.

This is the first indication on record of the diminishing

* Today, not only on the sea but even in the circus, men or women with tattooed faces are extremely rare. J. B. Johnson writes to me: "I have been hoping to obtain some photos of a chap billed as 'Van' who has been on exhibit in dime-museums in the East the past winter. Even his face and head are covered. I saw him in Philadelphia. This, so far as I can learn, is the only case in America where the face has been tattooed, although one tattooer told me that there are several men and one woman in Germany so decorated."

virility of the tattooing of the American sailors. After the World War the allegation that the American sailors and their skin-galleries are not what they used to be became common. In 1919 J. H. Taylor of the Identification Division of the Navy Department thus explained the decline of the puncture-art: "The men now being taken into the naval service are better educated and of a higher type, and are not superstitious like the old-time sailors." In 1927 in Los Angeles, Harry Lawson, tattoo-veteran of thirty-five years' experience in Norfolk, Honolulu and Californian ports, gloomily confirmed the decline, saying to me: "Them cake-eaters crowded the real men out of the navy." George Tichenor reported to me conversations he had heard in the foc'sles of many American freighters where young sailors would jeer old salts when the latter tried to show off their tattooings. A submarine electrician, a lad from Connecticut, informed me that tattooing was old-fashioned. By 1932 Bob Wicks was noting the decline of he-man patriotic designs among sailors: "Yes, the sailors don't care a thing for their country no more. Why, I tattoo flags and Miss Columbia on six soldiers for every one sailor. In the old days, a sailor was every bit as patriotic as a soldier, sometimes having flags and emblems on the back as well as the chest." On March 20, 1932, an anonymous writer proclaimed in the New York *Sunday Mirror*:

SAILORS ARE SISSIES! THEY USE POWDER AND COLD CREAM! And the Fight's All Out of 'Em, Adds Charles Wagner, Who Finds That Tattooing Has Been Eschewed by the New Breed of Sailorman!

Charlie denied with bitterness that he had ever said anything of the sort. He now claims that he never saw the tabloid writer and never spoke to him. "It ain't so," he protests, "if there was a jackie 'thout a piece of lucky tattooing on him, I'd know it." It isn't, says Wagner, that the

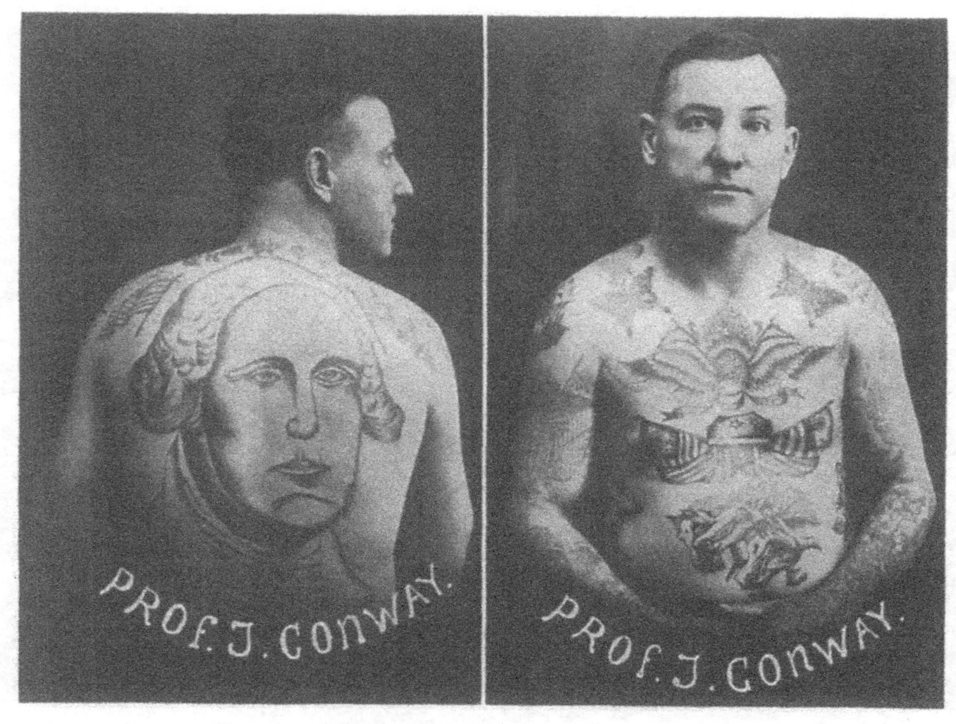

Front and back view of the patriotic motive.

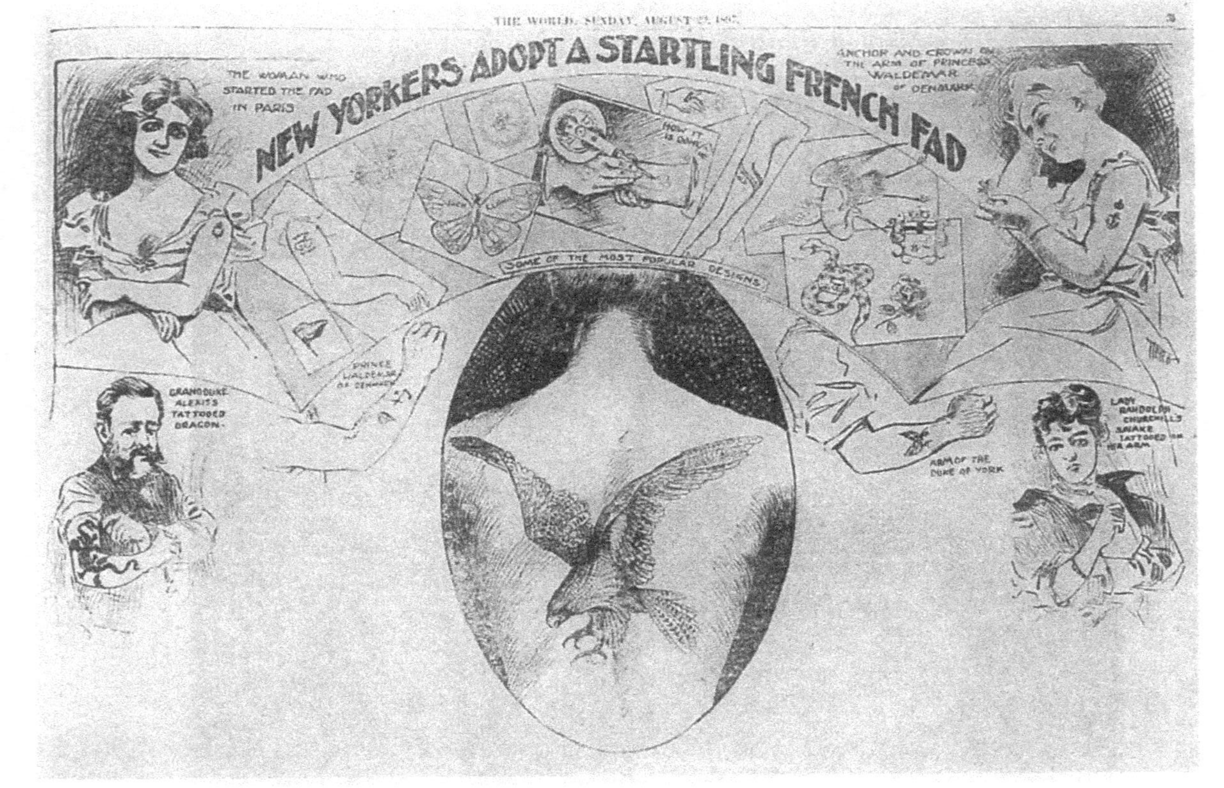

This illustration from the New York *World* reflects the height of the 1897 tattoo mania among high society. Note that the origin of the fad is here ascribed to France, rather than to England.

sailors

American sailors don't get tattooed because they don't want to. It is because the American merchant marine has been hit by the depression. The east coast tattoo-trade suffers especially because the Atlantic Fleet is in the Pacific, and has been there for the past several years. If anybody is to blame for the decline, therefore, let it be Mr. Hearst's Japan.

VIII

low herd—high society

1

THE herd motive in tattooing is particularly noticeable in a socially standardized country like our own. Quite naturally it was in particular evidence throughout the country during the last three major wars of the United States when hordes of men were brought together from civilian life into the barracks and told to take example in everything from the regulars.

But they were tattooed regulars. The tenderfoot therefore also blossomed forth with fair maidens, ferocious crocodiles and fancy fish. It was in a way an echo of the initiation ceremonial of a primitive tribe.

With soldier-tenderfeet, tattooing was also a short cut to bravery, a diploma of manliness, (much the same as with young warriors among the Maoris or Samoans) , but the herd motive was always stronger than this allied impulse. A former soldier who had served in Norfolk, Virginia, told me that if a man does not get tattooed right after entering the army, it is ten to one he won't get tattooed at all. His fears of not being considered a good soldier are allayed quite shortly after he begins his service, even if he has no tattooing on him. More soldiers are tattooed in ports, such as Norfolk, New York and San Francisco, than in inland points where they are not thrown into the company of sailors and marines, and the incentive of herd imitation is weaker.

As examples of the herd motive in tattooing, A. T. Sinclair related in 1908 that in one small district in Nova Scotia there was not a single man or youth tattooed. An old sailor came to live there, and within a year five hundred men bore the devices. The herd-imitation motive is a part of the identification process. Through the operation of tattooing, people strive to become identified with other people whom they happen to admire or envy.*

The first tattoo-fads among New York society in the early 1880's and 1890's were started in imitation of the tattoo-fads among European royalty and society. The British, Russian, German and Scandinavian heirs apparent, dukes, princes and princesses were tattooed mostly while they were junketing in their respective navies. They acquired epidermal dragons and flags in imitation of the seamen surrounding them. They wished to prove that they were good sports and brave sailors of royal blood. Thus the tattoo-habit, in several recurrent waves, came to American high society from the masses via royalty.

* A unique case of such herd-imitation tattooing was reported in 1876 by Martin Hildebrandt, of New York:

"About a year ago, a gentleman sent for me to come to him in a first-class hotel. He was a very handsome man, with as fine a style as I ever saw. 'Where to tattoo?' 'Right here,' said he, pointing to his face. 'I want you to put in a red band from my nose, on both sides, to the corner of my mouth—like a crescent—and I want a blue star on both cheeks and one in the middle of my chin.' I thought the man was crazy, and declined. 'Oh, I ain't out of my head,' said he, 'I am from the Indian Territory. I have been living among the Indians all my life, and a face with blue and red on it ain't a bit unnatural to me. It is a kind of necessity that I should get tattooed, so go ahead.' Well, as he kind of insisted I went ahead. I did my very best. It was good work and as true as a compass, and it suited him first rate. But I can't say it was pretty. It gave him an awful expression. Anyhow, he was satisfied."

tattoo

When the ruling classes go in for tattooing they are perfectly aware of the fact that slum-dwellers, toughs, sailors, and other plebs constitute the majority of the tattoo-fans in all the civilized countries. But they are not at all repulsed by this consideration. On the contrary, it is the subconscious desire of the upper class to borrow the primitive strength of the lower class. It is in line with the settlement work of the upper-class men and women in America and England. Three and four decades ago they went in droves to settle among the slum-people, ostensibly to help the down-trodden, really to help themselves to the tough fiber which they thought was plentiful among the poor. Others tried to borrow this same primitive strength by marrying their coachmen, chauffeurs, riding masters, chambermaids. In old Russia the aristocrats and upper middle-class men and women "went into the people," as the phrase was, not only to educate or propagandize them for a revolt, but also to improve their own stamina. Unlike the English and American aristocrats, the less repressed Russian aristocrats recognized their need for the toughness of the poor. When they "went into the people" they frankly spoke of the strength that "the soil" (i.e. the lower mass) was to give them.

In the lower American classes it is the men who get tattooed first and are then imitated by their women. In the upper classes it is most often the women who start a tattoo-wave and are then followed by their men. In society, while the fad lasts, women remain in the majority. This is not unrelated to the fact that it is the American society woman, more often than the American society man, who goes out to seek a mate in another nation, race, class—to infuse new strength into her race and class, to safeguard them against sterility and senility.

But in borrowing the tattoo-fad from the masses, London and New York society took care every time to identify themselves with their inferiors in the general spirit of the thing, not in its detail. They wanted to stamp their own aristocracy and wealth upon themselves. They insisted on different designs. They were obstinate about paying much higher prices to the tattoo-masters. The Mayfair denizens at times shunned the very term "tattooing" and employed instead the more aristocratic "tinting." They ordered their own coats of arms tattooed upon their skin, or the names and the emblems of their exclusive clubs, or reproductions of money-bills, or scenes of fox hunts in full cry. In America, rich men ordered the three nude figures of Wealth, Industry and Prosperity. In the early 1900's, Michael J. Butler, a Pennsylvania tattooer, moved to Baltimore and did a land-office business tattooing the dogs of the local Four Hundred with the initials, crests, and monograms of their owners.

2

On January 16, 1876 an anonymous writer in the New York *Times* related that some years before at a ball he had seen a charming young lady, on one of whose shapely arms a bit of lacy sleeve scarcely concealed a blue tattoo. The lady was the daughter of a distinguished American statesman from the South, the former governor of a State. His name was veiled in the account with a single initial C. Where did the beautiful lady get her blue mark? In North Africa, said the lady, where once, for a few hours she had been a prisoner of the Arabs. She thus described the process of tattooing:

She was completely disrobed, and an Arab costume forcibly put on her. An Arab woman delivered a smart blow to one of the girl's arms, and another Arab woman brought forward a small earthenware pot, from which some black substance was extracted and applied to the girl's arm. At this point the girl's father and other fellow-tourists arrived and claimed her without difficulty, for the Arabs explained away the whole affair as a friendly joke. However the girl's arm remained slightly sore for a day or two. The pain passed, but after a week the picture of a big blue butterfly, almost encircling the arm, came out in plain view, and thus, concluded the writer, "it was evident that the young lady had been tattooed for life with some Bedouin emblem."

This is one of the first cases on record of a member of American society being tattooed.* The same anonymous writer descended into Martin Hildebrandt's atelier in the slums of Oak Street, between Oliver and James Streets, and here learned that this worthy had been used to a considerable custom from New York society ever since the close of the Civil War. One may conjecture that men brought the tattoo-habit into their Fifth Avenue homes and clubs from the gory fields of the War.** Said Hildebrandt: "Sometimes I have been sent for to meet a whole company of gentlemen—yes, sir, men of style, living in handsome houses—and I have tattooed the whole lot of them—some private kind of mark, which I won't mention." From men the idea of tattooing spread to the women. To quote Hildebrandt: "Once two ladies called on me—real ladies. What did they want? Why, you wouldn't believe it! They wanted to have their cheeks

* The lady's explanation of the origin of her tattoo may have been but an ingenious fabrication. One cannot be tattooed by the magic process of a blow followed by the application of a black substance. The tattooing of a large butterfly, in those pre-electric days, would have taken more time than the lady allowed in her imaginative tale, and would not have occurred without the victim being fully aware of the nature of the operation. The governor's daughter was probably tattooed under prosaic circumstances by a more or less professional master, not against her will, but on her express order, and she must have paid a prosaic fee. But to heighten the awe produced upon her friends by the sight of the tattoo, to evoke sympathy instead of repulsion, she invented the romance of a strange adventure in Africa.

** Stephen Vincent Benét, in a recent letter to me, states that during the Civil War there were a number of tattooers in Washington, and that his references to tattooing in *John Brown's Body* he based on facts as recorded in diaries and other sourcebooks of the period.

marked red—with a kind of bloom. They offered me no end of money if I would try it, but I refused. I was not sure I could hit off the real color. Maybe if I had put on my color, and they had wanted to get rid of it, they would have abused me; for, once on, and ground into them, you must remember, it would have stayed there until their dying day."

It was about the same time—the 1860's and the 1870's—that the influence of English society men and women began to be felt here. The English patricians had been in the field decades before; many rich British brought from India some queer and indelible mementoes on their bodies. After India there came their acquaintance with Japan. The intricate, artistic tattooings of the Japanese intrigued them even more than the cruder Indian and Burmese patterns. English women of title and wealth followed their men. During the celebrated Tichborne trials of the early 1870's it was disclosed that twenty years before Roger Tichborne not only had been tattooed himself (anchor, heart, cross, and initials), but had also suggested the same operation to his girl-cousin.

In the summer of 1879 the London *Standard* carried an advertisement wherein reward was offered for the recovery of a young lady who had some time before disappeared most inexplicably. She must have hailed from the upper classes, for the advertisement listed much jewelry adorning her at the time of disappearance and mentioned a coronet on her linen. But what, on this side of the ocean, proved to be of most interest to the public was the advertised fact of a tattooed cross on the girl's left foot. Musing editorially on this tattoo, the New York *Times* (August 16, 1879) remarked: "From the way in which this assertion was made, it is clear that the fact of the tattooing was not regarded by the advertiser as anything unusual. In fact, from the comments since made by the English press, it is very evident that in England it is regarded as the customary and proper thing to tattoo the youthful feminine leg." The following January the same American journal estimated (perhaps echoing some English statistics) that "fully fifteen percent of the legs of—that is to say, at least seven and a half percent of fashionable London ladies are tattooed in inaccessible localities."

About the same time a journalist sent in from London, for the benefit of American readers, his dialogue with an English countess:

The journalist: But, how odd for a lady to be tattooed!

The English countess: I don't know, we pinch our feet like the Chinese and torture our poor waists with steel corsets; why should we not emulate the Indians and tattoo ourselves?

Another argument was also used: if the English girl is taught to pierce her ears and wear bits of metal in the wounds; and if she is encouraged to paint her face and dye her hair, why should she not be tattooed? Later, Andrew Lang, in his *Rhymes à la Mode,* proclaimed that a high-caste person, when tattooed, was really an Art's Martyr:

> . . . The china on the shelf
> Is very fair to view,
> And wherefore should mine outer self
> Not correspond thereto?
> In blue
> My frame I must tattoo.

On January 30, 1880, the New York *Times* explained the tendency of English society toward tattooing by the theory that the noble savage has become the newfangled ideal of the aesthetic Britishers, and that Walt Whitman's thunderings and Joaquin Miller's effusions shared with tattooing their popularity in England, and for the same reason:

> Mr. Walt Whitman and Mr. Joaquin Miller have achieved much popularity among cultured Englishmen not because they were falsely accused of having written

poetry, but because the physiological details of *Leaves of Grass,* and the piratical incidents told in Mr. Miller's wild Western verses, were supposed to be nature, with a capital N. The practice of tattooing, being a purely savage custom, suggests to the aesthetic Englishman the wild, free life of the isles of the "sun-down-seas," and hence to be tattooed is to put one's self in sympathy with Nature, and to protest against the sickly conventionalities of civilization.

3

But the mighty impetus to tattooing among English society folk and their American imitators was given not by any theories but by the circumstance that, on their trip to the Orient, two sons of the Prince of Wales happened to get tattooed. One of them was George, the present King of England. He and his brother, the late Duke of Clarence, acquired no more than a dragon on the arm each. But the newspapers of 1879 and 1880, both British and American, were full of reports that the tattooings were really broad arrows across the princely noses—the result of a midshipmen's prank. The London *World* was most lurid in these accounts, and the other newspapers reprinted and elaborated upon them. There was considerable consternation in the English palaces and among the faithful subjects, there was an indignant inquiry or two in Parliament. The princes returned from their cruise and the fears were allayed. There was no evidence of parti-colored noses. The reassuring news of the pretty and concealable dragons traveled quickly.

Faithful to their sovereign, the English nobility took up tattooing on an imperial scale. Beside the dragons, the coats-of-arms, the five-pound notes, and the pictures of fox hunts in full cry, they ordered upon their skin the emblems of their clubs and regiments, also representations of flowers after which the ladies of their hearts were named (Rose, Lily, Violet, etc.).

Members of the royalty and nobility of the continent followed the royal and noble islanders. In the 1880's and 1890's, the roster of tattooed rulers and their courtiers boasted: the Prince of Wales, later King Edward VII; his brother, Duke Alfred of Edinburgh and Coburg (Queen Victoria's second son); Edward's son, now King George V; George's elder brother, the Duke of Clarence (died in 1892); the Dukes of Marlborough, Manchester, and Newcastle; the Marquis of Salisbury; the Earl of Craven; Czar Nicholas II of Russia; the Grand Dukes Alexis (brother of Czar Alexander III), Constantine, and Michael of Russia; Queen Olga of Greece, the only woman-admiral in the world; King George of Greece (who had served as a midshipman in the British navy); Prince Henry of Prussia (brother of Kaiser Wilhelm); Archduke Stephen, of Austria; King Oscar of Sweden; Prince and Princess Waldemar of Denmark; Prince Victor Hohenlohe; Prince Christian Victor of Schleswig-Holstein; the Duke of Genoa (brother of Queen Marguerite, of Italy); Prince Jaime de Bourbon; Prince Phillipe de Caramen Chimay; Princess de Leon; and Princess de Sagan. There was a rumor that Kaiser Wilhelm, too, was tattooed, and on July 16, 1908, the *Australian Star*, of Sydney, remarked: "The German Emperor would look even more like a war-lord if we could behold the fearsome eagles on his manly bosom."

In the 1880's and 1890's, the continued tidings of the tattoo fad among the European olympians kept the fashion alive on this side of the Atlantic. As Sutherland Macdonald in London, so now Hildebrandt and Samuel O'Reilly in New York, all three outstanding tattooers of their time, began to feel the beneficence of the new royal pastime. At first Hildebrandt received the lion's share of society's business, for he had been a master of the needles ever since the middle 1840's and had a solid reputation. In August 1882 he revealed to the New York correspondent of the Kansas City *Times* that well-bred ladies from uptown had been coming to him in such numbers and paying so well that he was entertaining the idea of removing his shop from Oak Street to a fashionable uptown thoroughfare. O'Reilly was a comparative newcomer in the craft, having settled in New York only a few years back, in 1875. He was second only to the celebrated Londoner, Macdonald, in his suavity and persistence at furthering the new tattoo fad among the noble and the opulent. Gradually O'Reilly took over most of the custom among society people, and soon only a few remembered Hildebrandt.

But throughout the 1890's visiting English blue-bloods kept on remarking to their American hosts that in New York and elsewhere in the States there were no tattooers worthy of the name, that the London masters were only fair to middling, and that a trip to Japan was absolutely necessary for a truly artistic puncture.

The fame of Hori Chyo, a Japanese master of Yokohama, began to spread through the gilded mansions and exclusive clubs of the western world. On August 29, 1897, the New York *World* wrote: "Hori Chyo is the Shakespeare of tattooing because none other approaches him. . . . His lines are distinct as if they were made with the finest of delicate brushes. . . . Even the prejudice against the barbaric and senseless adornment cannot diguise the fact that (Japanese) design is one of art, and is executed with rare skill." Hori Chyo and other Japanese tattooers of the 1880's and 1890's were shrewd enough to advertise in guide books published in English. Visiting nobles and moneybags could find the tattooers attached to hairdressers' establishments, also to *les bains*, or to the so-called art galleries dealing in native antiques. Hori (i.e. the tattooer) Chyo was attached to the art-establishment of Messrs. Arthur and Bond in Yokohama. Later he boasted a charming bungalow on the Esplanade, with many young assistants softly moving about with pattern-books, needles and inks. All through the 1890's, despite the rapid introduction of the new electric tattoo-tools in all the major ports of the world, Hori Chyo and other Japanese masters continued at their hand-method, and even O'Reilly had to admit that their work was more artistic than the product of the best electric technique.

Hori Chyo's clients were greeted in excellent English. The master's business card had the engraving of three feathers and the rather familiar motto, "Ich dien," followed by these words: "Hori Chyo, tattooer by appointment to H. R. H. the Prince of Wales, H. R. H. the Duke of Clarence, H. R. H. Prince George, and to the Nobility and Gentry." It was he who tattooed Nicholas, the future Czar, then the Heir Apparent of Russia. Exquisite were the birds, the snakes, the dragons, the foliage, the Gods of Storm, and other designs placed by him upon his exalted British, American, and other Western visitors. Reverent and yet confident was his manner. So lifelike were his creations that once, at an aristocratic English gathering, a guest tried to shoo a miniature fly off his host's hand. The host, with proud laughter, explained that the fly was not a live one, but that it had been tattooed on his hand by Hori Chyo himself. Of Hori Chyo's largest pieces most renowned was a huge dragon covering, in three colors, the entire back of a rich American doctor.

In Kioto was another master who also boasted of highborn Western custom. He was engaged for a month reproducing on the trunk and limbs of an English peer a series of wondrous scenes from Japanese history, receiving for this about one hundred pounds sterling. He also tattooed the arm of an English prince, not to speak of the arms and shoulders of several English ladies. Among the pictures

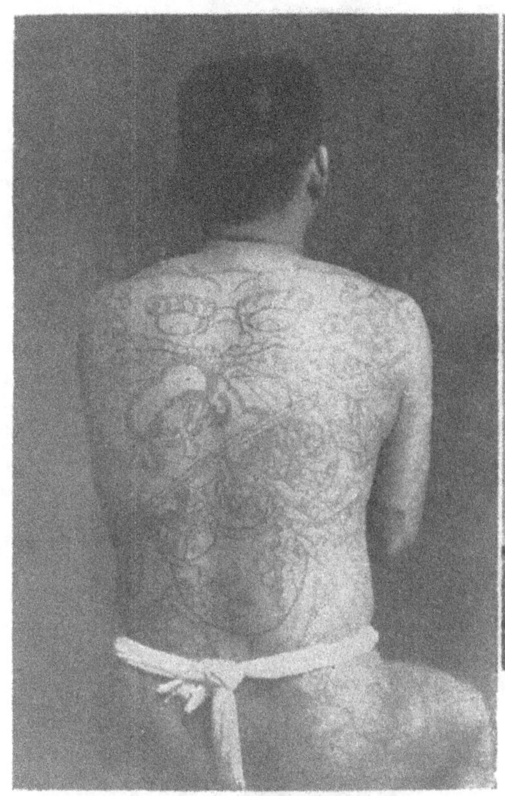

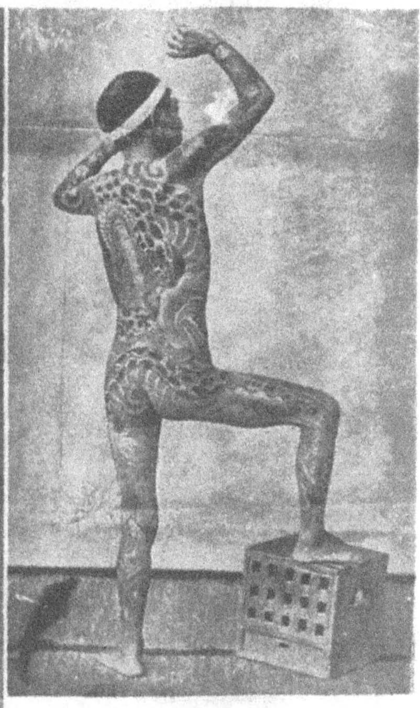

Tattooing in Japan

Japanese tattooing usually follows one of two general techniques. The picture on the left shows practically pure outline patterns, with very little or no shading. The second photograph exhibits heavy colored designs, luxuriant in chiaroscuro. Japanese tattooing on the whole has greater delicacy and aristic finish than the American variety.

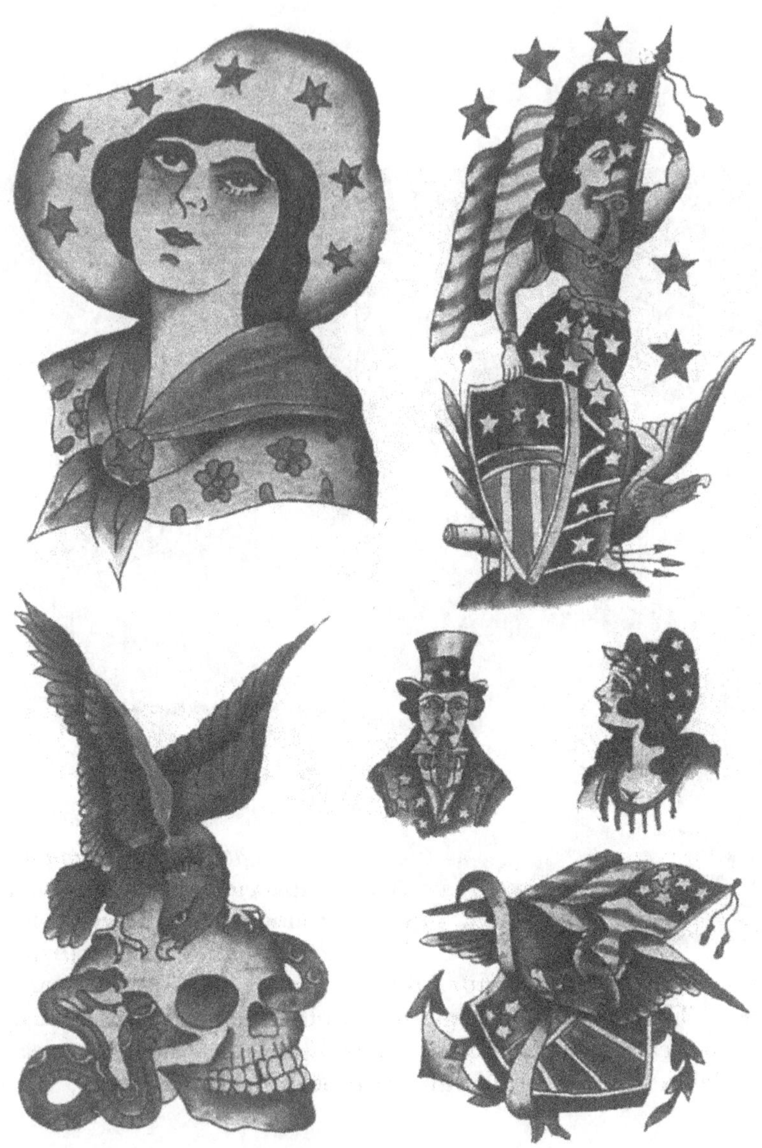

Conventional love-and-patriotism designs like these retain their popularity.

placed on this feminine skin he was particularly proud of one representing a tiny fan about the size of a halfpenny, on which there was a complete landscape with figures sharply outlined. In the late 1880's, hearing of prosperity in Hong-Kong, he repaired there, opening a studio and soon achieving an annual income of about 1,200 pounds sterling. As in Kioto, he cultivated in Hong-Kong the patricians' custom only, discouraging the visits of lowly drunken sailors by this English sign, hung in a conspicuous place: "I do not business if fuddled."

In Paris the Princesses de Leon and de Sagan said that they were tattooed by East Indian masters. In London, in the early 1890's, the branch office of a Yokohama tattooing establishment was opened, and from the very start received much patronage from aristocratic men and silk-stockinged ladies. Sensing big business, a certain Mr. Bandel, described as a millionaire from New York, offered Hori Chyo an engagement in America at an annual salary of $12,000. The tattooer was willing to migrate, but for some reason the deal did not materialize. Later, a few Japanese masters came to New York to become O'Reilly's assistants, but their stay in America was brief.

4

In the spring of 1893 the exclusive Racquet Club of New York was a-buzz with restrained excitement. A bath attendant and a member-bather were surprised to see the visiting Earl of Craven expose in all their vividness the crest of his house and other tattooed designs on his epidermis. The newspapers reported "some amazement and languid surprise as well as unfavorable comment at the Fifth Avenue clubs." The Earl of Craven chose to remain calmly aloof in the ensuing hubbub of outraged or amused voices, but his friends admitted freely that he was indeed tattooed. Other tattooed men were found among New York's clubmen. One of these men admitted that he had been tattooed while on a trip to Japan. He also volunteered the information that the summer before he had exhibited the beautiful specimens on his skin to his Newport co-loungers.

Cornelius Vanderbilt and other directors of the Racquet Club remained painfully silent amid all these gay admissions, but Ward McAllister, the arbiter of New York's Four Hundred, made this indignant statement to the press: "It is certainly the most vulgar and barbarous habit the eccentric mind of fashion ever invented. It may do for an illiterate seaman, but hardly for an aristocrat. Society men in England were the victims of circumstances when the Prince of Wales had his body tattooed. Like a flock of sheep driven by their master, they had to follow suit." He angrily revealed that some of the American clubmen had been tattooed, but did not feel at liberty to divulge their names. He blamed the phenomenon on the English influence. The newspapers noted that McAllister, despite the charges of un-Americanism often advanced against him, was a good patriot and was therefore free of any tattooings, those "decorations of the aristocratic Englishmen." Three years later another stronger voice was added to the protest against tattooing among the beautiful women of station. It was Professor Cesare Lombroso, who in 1896 cried out: "The taste for this style is not a good indication of the refinement and delicacy of the English ladies, for the custom is held in too great honor among criminals! We feel a genuine disgust! O Fashion, you are very frivolous; you have caused many complaints against the most beautiful half of the human race!"

In the ensuing recurrent waves of the fad in America, women usually took the lead, and the men followed. In

August 1897 the New York *World* quoted an anonymous English report that the tattoo-mania of 1892 had really come to England from America, and that three-quarters of the society women in America were tattooed. On December 12, 1897, the New York *Herald* demanded: "Have you had your monogram inscribed on your arm? Is your shoulder blade embellished with your crest? Do you wear your coat-of-arms graven in India ink on the cuticle of your elbow? No? Then, gracious madame and gentle sir, you cannot be *au courant* with society's very latest fad." The wave spread. O'Reilly made excited flying trips to Philadelphia and a few other cities to satisfy the high-born customers of those localities.

When newspaper reporters asked him for names, O'Reilly intimated that as a rule society people who were tattooed were proud of it among themselves but did not wish the world to know about it. He limited his talk to the disclosure of some of the rare designs he had placed on his New York customers. One woman, for instance, ordered from O'Reilly a horseshoe and a Ben Brush (a famous horse of the time). Another came with her own idea of a ladder upon which Cupids were gaily mounting. O'Reilly was somewhat hurt: "This woman never wears sleeveless gowns. I don't see why. Anybody ought to be proud of that decoration." But the names of the women did begin to leak out. Of the American women of fashion of a quarter-century and more back, Mrs. Jackson Gouraud, Princess Chimay and Mrs. George Cornwallis West became best known for their tattoos.

Mrs. Gouraud was born Amy Crocker, daughter of Judge E. B. Crocker, a San Francisco multi-millionaire. As a young girl she eloped with R. Porter Ashe, a nephew of Admiral Farragut. In 1888, after a divorce, she married Henry M. Gillig, commodore of the Larchmont Yacht Club. Then she met

Jackson Gouraud, an Englishman, a recent arrival in this country. In the spring of 1899 she sent her Japanese servant to the Chatham Square studio of Professor O'Reilly with a request to detail one of his Japanese assistants to her residence. O'Reilly sent Hori Toyo who on two separate occasions tattooed on Mrs. Gillig's arms a demon's head, a Japanese beetle, and two snakes, one twisted to make the initials "A. G.," the other, the initials "J. G." About the same time, Jackson Gouraud also sent for O'Reilly's Japanese artist, and had the same initials reproduced on his arm. Later Amy Crocker Gillig became Mrs. Gouraud. In her case we see the influence of her first two nautically inclined husbands combined with the English society influence of her third husband, all favoring tattoo as an ornament and an expression of sentiment. The fact that she had a Japanese servant, and that it was he who rode to Chatham Square to fetch a tattooer, is also significant. Perhaps he added his tales of the tattoo-marvels of Japan to the navy tales of her first two husbands and the society-tattoo chat of Mr. Gouraud.

Mrs. Gouraud proudly exhibited her tattooed arms at all the functions of New York and London, Paris and Newport, Nice and Cairo. So did Princess Chimay, born the daughter of a wealthy lumberman of Detroit. At balls she sported a snake around her right arm, just below the shoulder, and a striking butterfly on the shoulder. But Mrs. George Cornwallis West, formerly Miss Jennie Jerome of New York, and, at one time during her career, Lady Randolph Churchill, was more reticent. She preferred to conceal with a gold bracelet the snake, its tail in its mouth, tattooed around her left wrist. Only her best friends saw it.

Each wave of the fad would subside after a few months, to be revived two or three years later. In the 1900's and 1910's, whenever the fad returned, Professor Charlie Wagner,

O'Reilly's successor, donned soup-and-fish and stove-pipe, and got himself photographed in the act of covering some fashionably gowned society bud. Captain Burt Thompson, the Yacht Tattooer, cruising along the Atlantic coast, would tie up not only near the battleships and freighters, but also at the private beaches and near palatial yachts. During one of these waves of tattoo-popularity, it was rumored that a Chicago society woman had fallen in love with a Sells circus tattooed man, eloped with him, and at length got herself tattooed. If this is true it marks symbolically the height of the society mania.

After the World War Elsie French Vanderbilt married Paul Fitzsimmons, a naval officer of Newport, one of whose arms was grandly tattooed. It was her son William who, having entered the navy during the War, had first met him, and then introduced the lieutenant to his mother. The navy man subsequently beautified his name to Paul Fitz Simons, but the tattoos on his arm were left intact. It was about that time, or perhaps a year or two later, that polite American fiction began to concern itself with the tattoo-hysteria of high society. I refer the reader to Carl Van Vechten's *The Tattooed Countess.*

In the latest wrinkle, that of imitating tattoos on beach pajamas, the American smart set clearer than ever admits its debt to the sailorman. Miss Gwenyph Waugh, the creator of this fashion, says that her father has always loved and painted the sea, that her brother paints and gets wrecked in it and is a real connoisseur of the tattoos. But more than ever the smart set is snobbish about its acquirement of the low habit: it wears the sailorman's art not on its skin but on its sleeve, or, to quote a woman's page writer of a New York daily, ". . . the smart set can go in for all the tattooed heart and Venus decorations and all the butterflies and eagles that it wants—and come through the ordeal unscathed."

5

Caught between the sailor and the debutante, the middle-class American at times also uses tattoo to express his social mindedness. Tattooers report that it is the widespread custom in this country for the Masons, Elks, Rotarians, Odd Fellows, Shriners, Eastern Star women and other members of fraternal orders to have squares and compasses, horns, wheels, chains, crescents and sabers, stars and other formal emblems placed on their arms, chests or thighs. Not infrequently these designs are accompanied by mottoes expressing American clichés of Brotherhood, Service and Vision. A widely copied motif of social spirit, popular with the lower classes, is a tattoo-grouping of a cross, an anchor and a heart, the Faith-Hope-Charity design. An occupational design, such as a mechanic's hammer, a barber's razor, or a sailor's apprentice-knot (rope in the shape of figure 8), may also be interpreted as the man's desire to confirm his membership (and pride) in a definite social group. The New York *Tribune* of May 28, 1899, reported that an English railway official had a picture of a train going at full speed tattooed around his arm, in snake fashion:

> The scene is laid at night. The shades of evening envelop the snorting locomotive and flying carriages, while the rays of light proceeding from the opened furnace of the locomotive are effectively shown lighting up the cars. There are lights, too, issuing from the carriages, showing how the passengers inside are passing away the time. Some of them are reading, some sleeping, some talking, some sullenly looking out of the windows. A darkened portion of the train is passing the signal-box, and the dim light therefrom faintly lights up that part of the train.

That such a motive of occupational and social mindedness is often tied up with a deeper sexual motive can be seen from the fact that in some cases such designs, though not sexual in their outward themes, are placed near sexual organs. A tattooed representation of a ship's twin screws is not infrequently ordered by the sailors for their buttocks. A railroadman in Bayonne, New Jersey, has two trains emblazoned on his body: an engine on each buttock, a string of cars (freight, coach, and Pullman) running from the engine down each leg, to the very ankle.

Mottoes and designs of the type called "anti-social" by Professor Lombroso and W. D. Hambly, the English investigator, are rare in this country. Americans seldom order tattooings proclaiming their hatred of the authorities, their promise of revenge, their threat of death-to-the-bourgeoisie. For Americans, when they are criminals, believe in caution and would not provide the authorities with such tell-tale clues as anti-social tattooings.

In the olden times there roamed Americans tattooed as enemies of society, but the branding was done against their will. In 1818 the Massachusetts legislature passed a law that every second-term convict, prior to his release from the state prison, was to be tattooed on the inner side of the upper part of the left arm with the letters, "Mass. S. P." and the date of release. This was not by any means a new departure either in the application of tattooing or in the treatment of convicts. A. T. Sinclair remarks that branding for crime in New Hampshire, in the seventeenth and eighteenth centuries, was in fact tattooing. Tattooing as punishment and as a mark of crime had been known in England for many years before and after; it was practiced as such by many other races and tribes at many periods of history. The legend of the mark of Cain shows how far back it goes in the memory of man.

The most common reason assigned for a murderer's mark

was that it distinguished him as a fugitive from justice. Thus identified, he could be caught and punished. Also, people could see him for the criminal he was and shun him lest he do them harm. But Sir James George Fraser rightly remarks that the story of Cain implies quite the opposite: the mark was designed for the benefit of the murderer. It was meant to save him from the vengeance of his victim's kin, also from the wrath of his victim's ghost. One function of the mark was to disguise the murderer so that he could not be recognized; another, to make him so ugly and formidable in appearance as to frighten off the avengers.

The boastful anti-social tattooings found by Lombroso and Lacassagne on the bodies of their Italian and French subjects of study seem to support this theory. The tattooed criminals, through the terrifying pictures and bold mottoes, wish to frighten off their enemies. They order tattooed representations of the men they have murdered and the women they have raped. They think up scenes and mottoes blaspheming God and defying the authorities, swearing death to the bourgeoisie and proclaiming that they themselves do not fear death at all. "Executioner, when cutting, follow the dotted line" was a design around the neck of a French criminal. There are also designs and mottoes expressing self-pity, and calculated to evoke pity in others for their hard lives and tragic lot. Recently the Marseilles Scientific Police Laboratories reported that a man who had killed three of his comrades had a tattoo on him reading: "Born Unlucky." A Parisian apache had the picture of a guillotine tattooed on his back, with the self-commiserating inscription: "My last walk." A similar design on another man had the words: "Here's where I shall finish." On the back of a hardened murderer was the ingratiating motto: "Quick tempered but good natured." Those of the Parisian apaches and the Marseilles *nervi* who awaited their transportation to penal colonies, ordered tattooed pictures of such colonies with dolorous convicts in the foreground, inscribed "I shall soon be one of them."

Among the American criminals you will seldom find such clues to their anti-social pursuits as these blasphemous or death-to-the-authorities or I-am-bad designs. The American criminals are rather less imaginative or more repressed than the Latin criminals. Taking the period closely approximating the time of Lombroso's and Lacassagne's studies, and examining the tattooings of the American criminals of 1886, as listed in Inspector Byrnes' book,* I find in abundance such conventional designs as: simple dots, eagles, wreaths, American flags, square and compass, an Odd Fellow's link, figures and faces of women, names and initials, dates, lucky numbers, stars, bracelets, rings on the first or third fingers, shields, anchors, a very few crosses, a crucifix with a woman kneeling and a man standing up, the figure of a sailor with a flag, coats-of-arms, a goddess of liberty, clasped hands, a woman in short dress with a bow and a staff in her hand, an Indian queen mounted on an eagle, a full-rigged ship, hearts, mottoes such as "Love" or "You and me," etc.

Among the sixty tattooed men in Byrnes' list only one had as poetic a design as a sunburst, while another boasted a terrifying skull and crossbones. Neither blasphemy nor obscenity was reported. No threat of vengeance was discovered, nor any appeal for pity. One hundred and forty-four men and women, as against the sixty tattooed, had no designs on their skin listed as their distinguishing mark. No woman was reported as being tattooed but many Jewish criminals listed in the book had tattooings despite their strict religious prohibition.

Coming to the year 1933 and examining the photographs

* *Professional Criminals of America*, by Thomas Byrnes, New York: Cassell & Company, 1886.

of the bodies of the young delinquents on Randall's Island we see the same conventionality of design. We find Indian girls, sailors and sailor-girls, "true-love-to-mother," flags, coats-of-arms, horseshoes, horse-heads, eagles, crucifixes, crosses, hearts, initials, anchors. The nudes may be somewhat more frequent than in bygone days, also there are such "tough" designs as "death-before-dishonor" or daggers piercing the skin, but there is neither imaginative flight nor surly defiance even in such pictures.

In these modern days of gangsters and sawed-off guns, the police find, on a grassy Bronx lot, the body of Frederick Titus, alias Teti, put on the spot by his appreciative colleagues. He is identified not only through his fingerprints but also through the picture of a Red Cross girl on his left arm, inscribed: "Rose of No Man's Land," a dull conventional design—no "Executioner, follow the dotted line." In Lafayette, Indiana, in a strawberry patch the body of "Orlando Jack" Horton, a Chicago gangster, is found, apparently tossed from a speeding automobile. Identification is made possible by a necklace of playing cards tattooed around his neck. Such necklaces, as well as handcuffs (with a link or two broken) found tattooed around the wrists of some other modern gangsters, are the boldest anti-social designs found in America. The height of blasphemy was reached several years ago by Dorcas Deacon, alias Sally Scott, a Detroit gun moll, who, in addition to a "death-before-dishonor" design, had a serpent on her arm with the inscription: "The Godless Girl." The call for pity is evidenced by young delinquents when they say to their questioners that the symbols on their skin, I. H. S. (J[I]esus Hominum Salvator), really mean, "I Have Suffered," or "I Have Sinned."

IX

identification

1

"Why do I get tattooed? So they'll know me if I get bumped off," swaggers the sailor, the soldier, the thug. Thus runs the motive of identification through the variegated canvas of body-decoration.

Sailors in the early American navy used to tattoo, with gunpowder, their names as well as dates and birthplaces on their bodies. Lonely prospectors in the Southwest did the same, advancing the same reason. Frank Graf, the tattooer of Coney Island, tells me that he has customers for identification marks to be placed between their toes. They are bathers who presumably fear drowning and do not want their bodies sent to nameless graves.

It is not a bona fide motive. It is a pseudo-motive. It is the conscious, guilty rationalization of other, deeper and darker motives. It is, however, one of the most "honorable" of pseudo-motives for tattooings; it is easy to believe; it is often supported by actual cases of identification through tattoo marks, of the dead or of claimants to relationship and estates. Therefore, it is one of the most frequently given "reasons" for tattooing.

If there is a true identification motive in tattooing it is of quite a different sort. It is identification with the herd. It is also identification with a stronger being—the borrowing of his power through this magic of copying his tattoos or his image—in short, totemism. In identification with one's own self there is a certain element of narcissism. In love with themselves, these men and women order tattoo-inscriptions and designs highly individualistic, as much different from any other designs they have seen as possible, ostensibly to facilitate their identification in case of emergency, actually to express their love for themselves and their proud belief that they are different from other people.

All of us are narcisstic, points out Dr. Bromberg, and the reason why more of us do not go in for tattooing is that to the truly narcisstic the skin, this "sacred organ of the body," this "reservoir of narcissism," is "already perfect and endowed with all the glory and beauty of unadorned nature."

In other and paradoxical words, the tattooed are not truly narcisstic; their narcissism is a half-baked phenomenon that had no chance of flowering to its logical conclusion.

Their tattooing is a tragic miscarriage of narcissism.

2

Take the celebrated Tichborne case. In the spring of 1854 Roger Tichborne, a moody Englishman of means, perished in the sea, together with everyone else on the schooner *Bella*, bound from Rio de Janeiro to New York. In the middle 1860's a man appeared in Australia who said that Tichborne was not lost. The man said that he himself, a lowly butcher, was Roger Tichborne.

The butcher sailed for England and in a civil suit claimed Roger Tichborne's name and fortune. The suit started in London in May, 1871, and ended in March, 1872. So skilful was the claimant in his deportment and his earlier work of securing information about the Tichbornes that it took twenty-two days of questioning in the court to trap him in his lies. What really made the jury call a halt and caused the authorities to nonsuit the case and arrest the claimant for perjury was the testimony about tattoo-marks. It was clearly established that the real Roger Tichborne had been tattooed on the arm with the pictures of an anchor, a heart and a cross, and with the initials: "R. C. T." But the claimant was able to show on his skin none of these, and only the partly obliterated letters "A. O." could be seen on his body. He finally confessed that he was not the lost Tichborne, but Arthur Orton, a butcher's son from Wapping, England, whence, as a youth, he migrated first to South America and then to Australia. For his perjury he was tried in 1873 and 1874 and sentenced to fourteen years' imprisonment.

The case was much publicized, and its tattoo-climax gave an excuse for many Britishers, Americans, and Australians to acquire the craved body-marks without being ridiculed by their friends or plagued by their families. They could now point dramatically to Orton's unmasking and to the preservation of Tichborne's title and estate into rightful hands, all thanks to tattoos.

However, Tichborne was not tattooed because he wished to be identified in case of emergency. Tichborne's mother hated his father and loved her son with more than a normal love. She raised the boy as a sissified dandy. She was a Frenchwoman and the boy's English was peculiarly Gallic. He was made fun of by his English comrades. To prove to the herd his hardy manliness he acquired tattoos. The choice of designs was characteristic: an anchor to symbolize his fearless determination to go to the sea and thus disprove the sissy allegation; a heart to celebrate an unfortunate affair with his cousin (he thought he loved her when in fact he was doomed to a tie with his mother); a cross to denote the Catholic piety with which his mother had imbued him; finally, his own initials to signify the narcisstic self-love which dominated all his feelings and actions. His mother had told him how wonderful and different he was, later his comrades taunted him for his peculiarities; there was nothing else for him to do but to love himself as a person without parallel.

Orton had even less reason to tattoo himself for identification. His tattoos were less complicated. They were clearly of narcisstic origin. He was notoriously vain, dissatisfied with his early surroundings, proud of his daring, at times almost insanely convinced of his allegedly noble birth.

Take the Guldensuppe case. In the summer of 1897 parts of a man's body were found scattered in various sections of New York. The detectives working on the mystery noted that a tattoo-mark had been cut from the breast after the murder, as if to prevent the body's identification. They also noted that the soles of the dead man's feet were thick and rough, showing that he had been in the habit of going barefoot a great deal. Yet the soles were rather clean. This could mean only one thing: the man had been employed in a Turkish bath as a rubber. Detectives visited a few Third Avenue cafés frequented by Turkish bath employees, and here they learned that William Guldensuppe, a young rubber, had been missing for more than a week. He could be easily identified, for, since he had worked in the nude, everyone in the baths had seen a tattoo-mark on his chest. The body was identified as that of Guldensuppe's. A search was made among the dead man's associates, and the murderers were quickly found and convicted.

The Guldensuppe case was at the time, and for a long time after, hailed as an outstanding triumph of tattoo as a means of identification. The body could have been identified just as easily and the murderers found without the help of the tattoo, through the evidence of the soles and other numerous clues. But the missing tattoo mark on the dead man's chest was romantic and therefore heavily played up as the most important, if not the only clue to the victim's identity. Again, the tattoo-masters and tattoo-fans pointed to the importance of being tattooed for identification. But poor Guldensuppe, while acquiring his tattoos, had hardly thought of any such fate as proved to be his, and of providing a means of identification. His tattoo was a playing card, a symbol of toughness and recklessness, though aside from a liaison with a boarding house landlady his conduct was safe and modest enough. In his tattoo he sought a different identification, that with the herd of the slums, of the dives and gambling houses whose denizens were his customers at the Third Avenue baths.

Much of the talk of the importance of tattoos as a means of identification may be traced to the tattoo-masters and their desire to boost their business. In this respect their claims are at times fantastic. Even the American banking facilities are said to have benefited through tattoo as a handy and highly convincing means of identification. Louis Morgan, tattooer of San Francisco, wrote in 1912:

> A man traveling through Idaho recently had occasion to cash a check, but could find no one to identify him at the bank. After trying fruitlessly for some time to get proper identification he was about to give up when he remembered that his name and home address were tattooed on his arm. He went to the bank and showed the tattooing to the cashier, who then called the manager. It was then decided that no other person than he, who owned the name, would have had it tattooed on his arm so long before the check had been written, and so the money was paid over.

Bowery tattooers like to boast of the case of the finding of a long-lost father and how he was brought back into the family fold thanks to tattoos on his body. It took place in New York in May, 1914. Eleven years before a certain Mr. L. had lost his wife's and his own savings gambling in stocks. Afraid to face her, he vanished from his Yorkville home. But he went no farther than the Bronx. Here, he achieved the difficult feat of living as a hermit. In the meantime his family, too, moved to the Bronx, and in May, 1914, two of his daughters thought they recognized their father in a tumble-down hut not far from their house. A tattoo on his arm completed the identification. The children took him into their comfortable home where he learned that his wife had died only a few months before. "May God rest her soul," he said, "she was a good woman." He said that at one time, some seven years back, he, having recouped his fortune, tried to return to the family but found no trace of it.

One wonders, however, whether he did not all these years know just where his family was and just when his wife died, and whether he did not time his return and "tattoo-identification" to the day when he was no longer in fear of his wife. And had he not been tattooed not to provide a means of identification in case of need but to voice his manly protest against his wife by whom he was undoubtedly henpecked? His true "tattoo-identification" had occurred years before the fateful May, 1914. It was his identification, through tattoo and flight, with the world of men—venturesome, hardy, unafraid of women.

3

In fact, many of those men who get tattooed ostensibly for identification have good reasons to avoid just such identification. Far from the benefit that they are supposed to cause, the tattoo-marks as a means of identification may serve as an unwelcome give-away. This is true in cases where a criminal

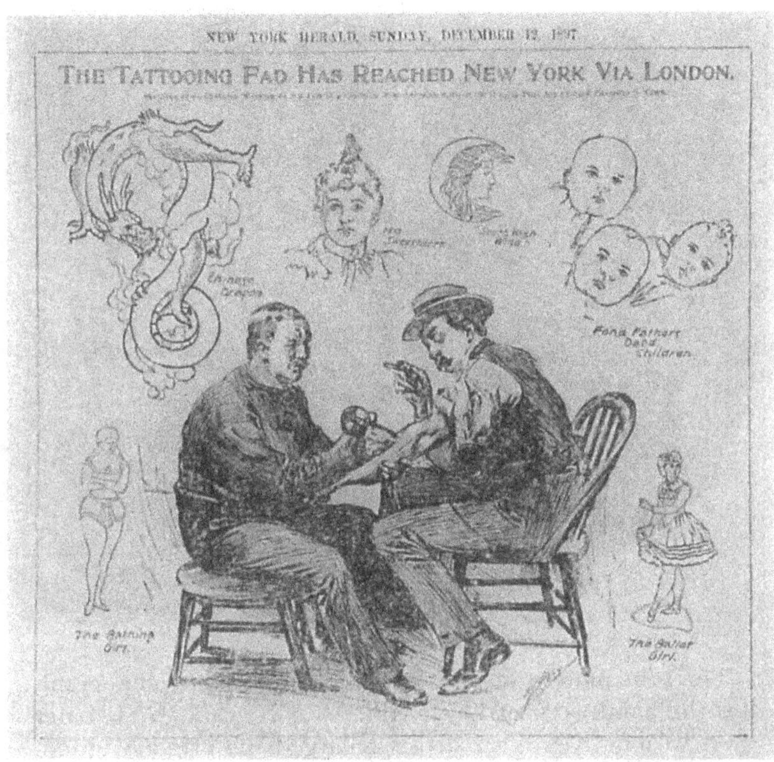

NEW YORK HERALD, SUNDAY, DECEMBER 12, 1897

THE TATTOOING FAD HAS REACHED NEW YORK VIA LONDON.

The operator here is supposed to represent Samuel O'Reilly, who during the 80's and 90's cornered most of the society tattoo trade in New York.

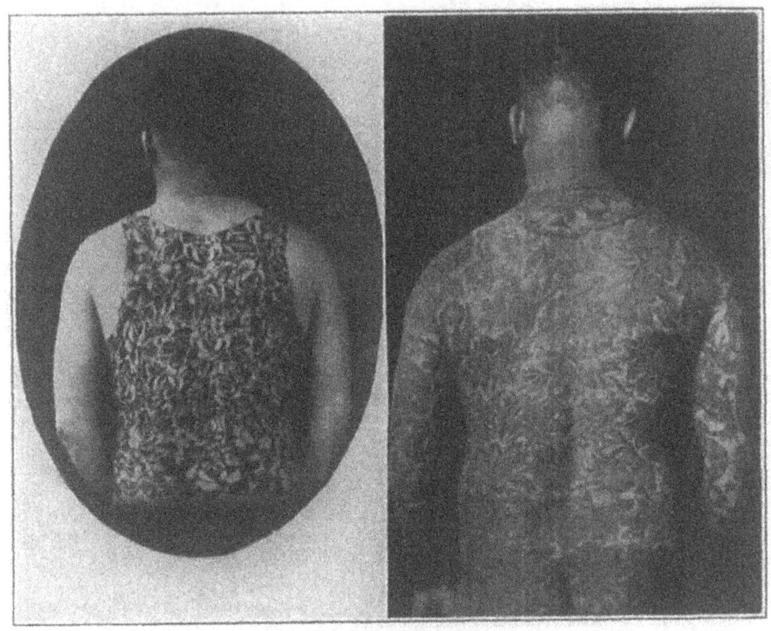

Tattooee's Progress

The neat pattern of roses displayed in the left photograph is the handiwork of Lewis Alberts of Newark, N. J. Later on various New York artists enlarged the original union-suit motif until the complicated result shown in the right-hand photograph was finally reached. Before he was finished this gentleman was tattooed everywhere (including the soles of his feet) except on his hands and face.

is not done away with by his enemies but is very much alive and does not wish to be identified when captured and grilled.

The tattoo-marks are also a give-away when a man deserts from the army or the navy. The British admiralty has for decades kept a most minute record of all the tattoo-marks to be found on the bodies of enlisted men. Sometimes military authorities discourage tattooing in order to guard from the enemy the identity of the fighting units. On February 5, 1918, in Spartansburg, South Carolina, Major-General O'Ryan of the Empire Division forbade tattooing soldiers' skin with the names, numerals and other insignia of their regiments, explaining that when the men go into the trenches, the tattooed privates would be useless for patrol work.*

That the pseudo-reason of identification advanced by those who get tattooed was rather threadbare was realized as early as 1879, when the New York *Times* ridiculed editorially the custom of young society women in England to be tattooed against their own disappearance:

> May we not . . . assume that English girls are prone to stay away from home, and that being so very numerous, they are frequently mislaid or forgotten? The careful British parent desires to mark his girls for identification. If he pastes labels on their backs or attaches tags to their belts, the tags and labels can readily be torn off or lost. To brand a girl with a hot iron, or to slit her ear, practices which are in vogue among cattle-drivers, would

* Indeed, any sort of tattooing may be a damaging evidence in time of war. Billy Donnelly tells how during the World War two Scotland Yard detectives, with a suspect handcuffed to them, visited his Southampton studio. The prisoner insisted he was a Russian and had never been in Germany. Donnelly looked at the tattooings on his body and announced them definitely German. He said they were done in Hamburg and even named the master. Amazed, the prisoner admitted that he was a German spy and soon was convicted as such. (Somewhat similarly there are stories of identifying amnesia-sufferers not through the subject matter but through the styles and geographic origin of their tattoos.)

> obviously be open to serious objection. The careful parent, in these circumstances, falls back upon tattooing, and in order not to disfigure his girls, he has them tattooed where the indelible mark is not, as a rule, constantly forced upon the public gaze.

The editorial funmaker assured his readers that the advantages of the custom were undeniable, and cited a couple of mythical cases:

> Let us suppose that the girls of the Smith family, for example, are marked "S" in a diamond. Now, if old Mr. Smith, when taking his nine girls to Brighton, mislays one in the railway station, or forgets another and leaves her in a cab, he has merely to advertise that on such a date a girl marked "S" in a diamond was lost or mislaid in such or such place, and she will soon be restored to him. Or suppose that the same Mr. Smith finds a girl in an omnibus whom he fancies belongs to him, but whom Mr. Brown rightfully insists is his private girl. There need be no dispute about the matter. Mr. Smith has only to say to Mr. Brown, "How are your girls marked?" Mr. Brown replies "J. B." with a star. An inspection of the disputed girl shows that Mr. Brown is right, and there is at once an end of the dispute. Thus, we see that tattooing a girl as a means of identification might be a very useful practice, and . . . it commends itself to our approval. . . . Whether the custom will be introduced here remains to be seen—of course, by qualified and legitimate eyes. Probably, it will gain ground slowly among us for the reason that girls are not so abundant here as in England, and the danger of losing them is, therefore, comparatively slight. (The New York *Times*, August 16, 1879.)

The identification reason for tattooing may be considered as less subject to ridicule when the tattooed are children.

Children, indeed, may be forgotten and lost in cabs, omnibuses, stations and other conveyances or public places, or, coming to more modern times, kidnapped by gangsters. American tattoo-masters reported a brisk business in the marking of children in the spring and summer of 1932, at the time the Lindbergh baby was kidnapped. There is a wave of such tattoo-orders each time the newspapers run scare headlines about the kidnapping of a baby. Again, there is a mild wave of tattooing the newly born babies each time the newspapers report an accidental exchange of babies in maternity hospitals. Charlie Wagner says that a certain maternity hospital in Manhattan has been negotiating with him to tattoo all the babies there immediately after birth, to avoid the mix-up in babies so feared by mothers. A few years ago, a certain young British countess had her two newly born twin sons tattooed with two different marks to ensure one of them, older by a few minutes, his right to the ancient Scottish earldom and vast estates.

There is more of seeming justification in such cases than in the many cases of adult tattooing-for-identification. And yet again, even in these cases of tattooing the children, there is much more than the "simple" and "honorable" motive of identification. There is the subconscious drive of incest undoubtedly governing those parents who order tattooings on their children's skin. As to the results, the evil element in such tattooings by far outweighs the identification-benefit that may accrue in cases of kidnapping or of succession-arguments. What deeply-hidden fears of castration, and consequently of hatred for the parents, these "identification"-tattoos may not start in the children, pursuing them far into their wrecked and wretched adult lives!*

* For a more detailed discussion of the castration complex and other problems of the tattooed young, see Chapter IV.

4

Not only men, women and children, but animals and poultry as well are tattooed in America for the purpose of identification. Butler's work of tattooing rich ladies' dogs with the monograms of their owners (Baltimore, the early 1900's) was the beginning of this phenomenon. On July 10, 1915 the New York *Evening World* revealed that the Adams Express Company at one time had some of its horses tattooed (rather than branded in the regular manner of hot iron), but that later it discontinued this practice. The tattooers of New York reported at the time that dogs were most frequently tattooed on their noses, with crosses, numerals, or owner's initials, while horses were tattooed on their underlips with numbers or special figures. "This," wrote the *Evening World*, "sometimes confounds the horse stealer." In 1926 Charlie Wagner received the custom of a Staten Island dog fancier who had had one of his blooded hounds stolen from him and therefore had all his other dogs tattooed with certain marks under their forelegs.

The tattoo method of marking hogs has been repeatedly recommended to farmers and stockyards by the United States Bureau of Agriculture. In the fall of 1932 the Milwaukee *Journal* printed the news that in the Northwest silver-gray foxes have been brought to the tattooers' studios to have initials or trade-marks punctured and inked in the smooth lining of their ears as a means of identification in case of theft.

In the summer of 1927 tattooing of turkeys was adopted in the vicinity of San Angelo, Texas, because of many recent thefts. A produce dealer of Paint Rock claimed to have invented and patented an electric needle process especially to tattoo poultry. Each turkey raiser reserved a special brand,

and all the tattoo-brands were duly registered with the county clerk. In the summer of 1932 tattooing of chickens and hens was adopted by the Caroline County (Maryland) Poultry Association as a means of combating fowl stealing. On April 3, 1933, Colonel H. Norman Schwarzkopf, superintendent of the New Jersey state police, announced in all solemnity that an identification bureau for tattoed chickens will soon be established by his office. A system similar to automobile registration will be used, each county given a letter of its own, and any poultryman allowed to tattoo his birds on the left wing and then register his particular mark with the bureau. Colonel Schwarzkopf, who is remembered for his unsuccessful search for the Lindbergh baby and its kidnappers, explained that the main idea is "to make chicken stealing more hazardous."

Tattooing of poultry against theft has now spread from America to a score of other countries. In the Argentine, for instance, the tattoo marker is being used not only against theft but also for keeping records in laying contests and recording of fancy breeds and show birds.

But again, one wonders how well even those who tattoo their animals and poultry against stealing know their true motives for such acts. Of course they would indignantly refute allegations of sadism or sodomy, however subconscious, as explanations, however partial, of this phenomenon. But there is no doubt that identification-against-loss as a reason for tattooing men and animals is not a reason, or at least not the only reason for the act, no matter how honestly and sincerely men may advance such a reason. At best, if not a hint of sadism, incest or sodomy, it is a manifestation of one's love for oneself—for one's offspring and possessions—a manifestation of narcissism.

X

faith, magic, and disease

1

TOTEMISM was one of the chief motives of tattooing among the American Indians. The figures of animals tattooed on their bodies were the symbols of their totems—their protectors, the suppliers of a magic power. But the many religious and magic-invoking designs in the tattooing of white Americans do not owe their inception, in any noticeable measure, to the totemic tattooing of American Indians. These designs can be traced to the early days of the Anglo-Saxon world. Among the dawn Christians of England the custom of tattooing holy designs on the body was so widespread that in 787 A. D. a council in Northumberland voiced its alarm and prohibited the practice. The Irish monks of the distant past were tattooed extensively. But the greatest impetus to the phenomenon was given by the pilgrims to the Holy Land.

It was, and still is, the custom for a Christian pilgrim, shortly after his arrival in Jerusalem, to have a religious symbol, or a whole series of them, tattooed on his chest or arms. The custom is said to have been introduced by Armenians. The name or initials of the pilgrim and the date of his pilgrimage were added in many cases. The earliest English pilgrims to the Holy Land followed this custom. As in the totemic tattooing of the Indians there was a certain element of sacrificial masochism in the tattooing of these holy Christian designs. The pain of the operation would ensure the mercy of the divine powers. More practically, the pilgrims hoped that such marks would impress the inhabitants of the countries through which they had to pass and would make their passage safe, or, if the worst should overtake them, the tattoos would serve as their identification marks, ensuring them Christian burial. The belief in the protective power of the pilgrims' tattoos spread in England; the religious designs were adopted by non-pilgrims as well; from England these designs were brought to the colonies, America among them.

The Puritans interfered with the spread of the imported custom, just as they frowned on native Indian tattooing. Had they been allowed to do so, the Indians would have strengthened the imported holy tattooings by sharing their own totemic opulence with the white newcomers. When, in the third quarter of the eighteenth century, Bossu, the French explorer, visited the Arkansas (Quapaw) Indians, they tattooed his thigh with the sign of a roebuck. It was a sacred and joyous ceremony. The Quapaw told him that all their allies would welcome him as brother when he showed his mark. They, as well as a number of other Indian tribes, were ready to accept the paleface men as their totemic brothers in the name of tattoo. But the stern Puritans of New England, and not the smiling French visitors, proved the dominant influence on the new continent. The Puritans considered the Indians veritable children of the Devil. The Puritanic stress was on the Old Testament: "Ye shall not make any cuttings in your flesh for the dead, nor print any marks upon you." (Lev. XIX. 28). Thus the Puritans from the very start combated Indian tattooing. The Christian missionaries among the Redmen (and later among the South Sea Islanders) did much to discourage the native tattoo art. In old New England tattoo came to be the mark not of holiness but of black arts and crime. It was Cain's mark. Basically it was a mode of adornment to be warred upon by the unsmiling, unornate Puritans.

American seamanship, rapidly developing in scope and free spirit, gave due battle to Puritanism. Sailors began to bring magic designs from the Far East and South Seas and religious tattooings from the Near East. Sailors were at the constant mercy of the elements; they needed these tattooings as a means of propitiating the angry powers that caused storms and drownings and disease far away from shore.* In 1908 A. T. Sinclair noted: "A large proportion of our naval officers at some time visit Jerusalem, and I have never been able to hear of one who did not conform to the usual custom. One petty officer, a first-class yeoman, was the only exception. He told me that he should have been tattooed but did not have time." Today, as in the days of the early pilgrims, swastika crosses, plain crosses, crucifixes, biblical scenes and religious mottoes are tattooed upon the Americans, sailors and non-sailors, not only because these customers wish to express their unselfish piety, but also because they believe that such religious designs on their skin will ward off evil, prolong their lives and stand them in good stead on the Day of Judgment.

Also, as in the days of early pilgrims, there are known today, in America and other white man's countries, cases where the tattooed do not believe in the magic power of their designs but trust that their enemies, actual or potential, will believe in such powers and thus be restrained from attacks upon them. In 1898 Frank Howard revealed to his inter-

* This, of course, in addition to the already discussed homosexual motives.

viewer: "The man that goes into the Wild West or Northwest pioneering gets tattooed because the Red Man has a superstitious regard for an inked-in design on a man's body." Sutherland Macdonald told of tattooing hideous and frightening designs, mostly devils, on the body of a man going into the wilderness of Africa. The man expected to impress the natives with the idea that he was in league with supernatural forces, and therefore could not be attacked. Frank Graf tells me of a New York man who ordered a will tattooed on his back. The man hoped to awe his family into immediate and unconditional acceptance, to exclude any possibility of his children going to court and contesting.*

2

Today, the three most popular religious designs among the American tattoo-addicts are: the Rock of Ages; Christ on the

* Tattooing of wills on men's and women's backs is not infrequent among the Americans and the English. Besides the desire to make a will magically irrevocable and uncontestable, there is a certain exhibitionist motive involved. Not all such will-bearers are as surprisingly lucid in their explanations as Graf's customer. Usually, they tend to rationalize the tattooing of wills. Thus, there are stories of prospectors who anticipate a sudden or violent death somewhere in the desert and want these wills on their backs as identification of their mortal remains and to ensure a proper disposal of them. Tattooer Jim Wilson, formerly of Brooklyn and now of Panama, loves to tell the story of a father and a daughter who were shipwrecked on a lonely isle. The man was rich and wanted to make sure that his daughter, in case of his death and her survival and rescue, would get all his money. Therefore, with shells and blood of cuttlefish, he tattooed his will on her back. Jim Wilson's story is undoubtedly a corruption of the plot of *Mr. Meeson's Will,* a novel by H. Rider Haggard. Legal complications of such documents are rather interesting. In 1917, there died in Pittsburgh one John Ballantyne Hood, who had on his back his tattooed will, "All my earthly possessions I bequeath to my beloved mother." A high official in the Register of Wills ruled: "If there were two witnesses who can be found who saw the will made, or two witnesses who heard Hood say that he desired his mother to have his estate, such will could be proven. If no such witnesses are found then the will is what is called a destroyed will. The fact that it is on his back and was undoubtedly tattooed there by his order does not alter the case".

cross; a cross with a legend, "Dear Mother," or "To my Mother."

The Rock of Ages cross is a favorite with sailors and usually has a naval background, such as a sailship in full billow. The crucifix is often supplied with an additional touch of two angels ministering to Christ. The mother-cross frequently has a weeping willow behind and above it and a melancholy tar in front, slightly to the right. There is also a cross emerging from a red rose; or a cross with a flaming heart in its middle, a royal crown encircling its lower extremity. Some mother-crosses are accompanied by girl-angels of paradoxically voluptuous aspects. Among thousands of American tattoo marks examined, I have found very few crosses dedicated to dead fathers.

Less frequent, yet persisting, are such designs as: St. George on horseback with a long spear directed at a vanquished dragon on the ground; Madonna with the infant Jesus; Peter and the crowing cock; the infant Jesus with angels looking down at Him from the clouds; the head of Jesus in the crown of thorns; Jesus bearing the cross, the Holy Spirit descending in the form of a dove; churches; incense lamps; church candelabra. A variation of a crucifix is Al Neville's design: a naked girl crucified on a dagger, her hands tied to the handlebars with nautical ropes.

The erotic motif emerges clearly. Witness the voluptuous girl-angels, the flaming hearts and red roses and other feminine designs pierced by phallic crosses, or the frankly sexed girls crucified on dagger-crosses. The sadistic-masochistic elements of the erotic motif are evident from St. George's spear aimed at the dragon, from the many and various figures of suffering Christ, suffering sailors weeping in front of mother-crosses, suffering St. Peter. Thus the basic nature of tattooing colors even the supposedly ascetic religious designs.

The costlier and more elaborate tattooings are those of the

Last Supper and the Lord's Prayer. These are ordered by persons who have had "visions," also by professional tattooed men and women performing in circuses or dime-museums. In 1927 Dr. Shie reported a case where beneath the Last Supper, occupying the entire back of a man, were the really touching words: "Much obliged to Joe." Joe was a generous friend who had paid the high fee for the tattooing. One of the best reproductions of the Last Supper is that on the back of Princess Beatrice, an American circus performer, with an admonition in large letters; "Love One Another." Jack Redcloud, the showman-tattooer, has a picture of Christ tattooed on his head which he keeps shaven while on the road. Martin Jensen, a circus performer, acquired from Wagner one of the most elaborate Madonnas known among the tattooed: the Holy Virgin, in standing pose, surrounded by thirty-two angels, occupying Jensen's entire back. Recently Wagner completed "The Celebration of the Fiesta of Our Lady of Mount Carmel" on the back of Thomas Lee, a longshoreman, a native of Edgewater, New Jersey. It has twenty-three angels, many fleecy clouds, and a number of trumpets which seem to blow the glory of Charlie. The tattoo is a yard wide and a yard high; it is done in red, yellow, brown, purple, two shades of green and two shades of red. To quote "Slick" Russell, another tattooer and Charlie's admirer, this particular tattoo is a masterpiece, being "like the sun in the sky, like a window in the church, like the foam on a stein of British ale." To keep up with his name, C. E. Church, a circus man, commissioned Dad Liberty of Boston to cover his back with a copy of the Madonna and Child. The job took four months and cost Church several hundred dollars. Generally prices depend on the fervor of the client and the size of the design. "I can do a Rock of Ages for $1.50, but if a man is real religious I can do one on his back for $150," remarks Bob Wicks obligingly.

In the large sizes and high prices of religious tattooings among the circus people we see at work the familiar complex of guilt, the desire to gain absolution of the tattoo-sin (and of the sinful exhibition of tattoos) by making these tattoos religious, large, and costly. No spectator, however pious, could object to the exhibit's tattoos when these tattoos testified to the piety—and pious masochism—of the exhibit. But Joe who paid for the Last Supper on his friend's back was in fact sadistic rather than generous, seeking an absolution of his own obscure guilt through his friend's suffering. Joe may have had a "vision" but shunned the physical pain of the tattoo-operation. The nearest he could come to a circus-man's masochistic sacrifice was to make the Last Supper large and costly, and foot the bill. The same guilt-absolution-seeking may be the main motive of those tattooers who sadistically inflict extensive religious tableaus on the backs of the willing longshoremen, or rave about such masterpieces.

An interesting example of the Lord's Prayer was discovered in a San Francisco hospital, early in this century, on the back of a sick sailor. He hailed from Nova Scotia, from a devout family. His mother, on her deathbed, had asked him never to part from the back cover of the family Bible with the Lord's Prayer printed in golden letters. For many years he carried the cover. One day, in a fight with a fellow deckhand, he accidentally dropped it overboard. From then on, many misfortunes visited him, and he attributed them to the loss of the Lord's Prayer. Once a sailor interrupted his tale of woe to suggest that the unfortunate man have the Lord's Prayer tattooed on his back: "You'll never lose it, my hearty." The sailor gladly followed the suggestion, ordering the best job of the Prayer available, and behold! his troubles ceased. Here again we have an example of a masochist-exhibitionistic craving glossed over by the double excuse of: 1. love for mother, obedience to her last will and command; 2. religious nature of the tattoo.

Somewhat similarly, love for kin combined with deep piety may serve as an excuse for the sadistic infliction of a tattoo. Such an example was reported in July, 1895 from Ellis Island. A tall, handsome French machinist, answering to the name of Eugene Boussard, alighted from a ship. The immigration officials noticed that he wore his hair low down over his forehead. Asked for the reason, he raised the hair. Across his forehead was the tattooed motto: *"Dieu est mon Berger, je n'aurais besoin de rien!"* (The Lord is my shepherd, I shall not want.) The young man said that a religious aunt of his had caused the verse to be tattooed on his forehead when he was a boy of twelve.

The younger generations of immigrants in America, unsure of the reaction of their elders, or of the better-class native-stock outsiders, to their newly acquired tattoos, also seek to acquit their deeper motives by selecting pious (almost missionary) designs. In New York and other large American cities, the most numerous orders for religious tattooing have been recently coming from Italian youths and men. In addition to the crucifixes, the increasing practice is to bring the pictures of their patron-saints to be reproduced on their arms and chests. Spaniards and Puerto Ricans in New York and elsewhere have been still more recently following the Italians in the same custom. A singular case was reported in Brooklyn some thirteen years ago. An Italian boy of fourteen was filing a knife when it slipped and penetrated his heart. He was rushed to a hospital where the doctors said that the knife had not gone far enough to kill him. While the boy was in the hospital, his family and neighbors prayed for him at a shrine of the Sacred Heart. Naturally the boy's family and neighbors, as well as the boy himself, explained his recovery as the result of the prayers. When he was up and about, he, accompanied by his parents, came to a tattooer and ordered a picture of the Sacred Heart tattooed across his chest.

Among religious mottoes, unattended by pictures, "Ecco Homo" is the leader. On the throat of John Solinsky, a Pennsylvania Pole, I found the two words: "Jesus Saves." Here is clearly a "missionary" excuse for an extremely pain-pleasurable operation on a sensitive part of the body. A religio-political missionary spirit is the excuse for the tattooing of swastika crosses. Of late swastika crosses are growing in popularity as luck-evoking tattoo marks. Charlie Wagner tells me that the Italian immigrants were the ones to introduce swastika into American tattoo-lore. The very word *swastika* is as yet a tongue-twister for an American tattooer. Usually he says: "Aw, you mean the cross that's on them taxis." Lately, for some obscure reason, the American tattooers call the swastika symbol "that weegee cross."* When reversed, the swastika cross is supposed to bring bad luck. Wagner says that in one case he had to surcharge a reversed swastika with a flower, and then tattoo a correct swastika on another part of the body. The customer was vehement as to the misfortunes which the reversed "weegee" had brought him, an honest American seaman. But then an error in any design is generally supposed to bring bad luck to the tattooed. Fearing the unknown and the irregular, unable to fathom and interpret it, man clings to a straw and ascribes his misfortunes to minor deviations from his routine, deviations totally unrelated to his major problems.

Swastika crosses bring us to the Jews. The Jews in America, though contributing their quota to the ranks of tattoo-fans, are not responsible for any special religious or superstitious designs. Far from being an incentive to, or an excuse for tattooing, the Jew's religion keeps him from it. There was

* Old-time ouija boards were often decorated with swastika crosses. Thus, "weegee" is perhaps the American folk corruption of "ouija."

the case of a Jewish young man, a racketeer and speakeasy owner in New York, who had on his left arm the tattooed portraits of his children, a boy and a girl, done in profiles turned away from each other. One day, in conversation with a rabbi, he revealed these decorations. The rabbi was aghast. He told the young racketeer that he was doubly an outcast from the Hebrew faith. To be tattooed on the right arm or any other part of the body was bad enough, but to desecrate the left arm was doubly bad, for it is on the left arm that a good Jew winds his phylactery.

According to one theory, the trail leads back to the mark of Cain. A tattooed person wears the mark of Cain; he is an outcast from the society of his fellow-men. It is the fear of leaving the tribe, probably the strongest factor in the adhesive tendency among Jews, that finds a symbolic representation in their religious taboo against tattooing. It is probable, remarks Dr. Bromberg, that some such feeling runs through the minds of all those who are tattooed. "In the sense of Jung," writes Dr. Bromberg, "the unconscious of the individual carries in it the taboos and fears of the race; the 'collective unconscious' of all of us carries the taboo against tattooing, against taking on the mark of Cain."

Lew-the-Jew says that he has always been conscientious toward his co-religionists as his customers. He says that in his career he has warned many a Jew, who bared his skin before Lew's needles, of the Mosaic law. Many an American-Jewish youth would evince utter astonishment when told of the prohibition. Many would hear of it for the first time in their lives, and, fearing to bring their elders' wrath upon themselves, would withdraw from Lew's establishment with no pictures executed on their rinds. Lew lost a considerable amount of business in this manner, yet his principles came before profits, says he. Not satisfied with his own scrupulousness he insisted that his Gentile co-professionals act the same way, and many did.

I hear, however, that this warning has had slight effect of late. Second-generation American Jews seem to care little about the Mosaic anti-tattoo law or their parents' ire. They want tattoo pictures on their skin, and it's nobody's business but theirs whether or not they have those beautiful geishas, big butterflies and full-rigged ships on stomach and thigh. True, there is many a Jew like the news-vendor of Lawson's clientele who ordered "Harry-Goldie-June," (respective names of his favorite Jewish prize-fighter, his wife and his little daughter) inscribed on his skin, and who still has to hide his tattooed arm from his pious mother. But there are also many Jewish sailors on all American coasts and many Jewish salesmen, truck-drivers, chiropractors—and even lawyers in many American cities, who do not have to report their morning ablutions to their mothers. The Jewish clientele of the American tattoo-craftsmen is, generally speaking, on the increase. Here we see in operation the general tendency among the Jews to be assimilated, to be American, to prove their manly hardiness to those non-Jews who are apt to talk of the Jews' alleged fear of risk and pain. It is in part the herd-imitation motive that brings some second-generation lower-middle-class Jews of America into the ranks of the tattooed.

As a matter of fact, were they better versed in the Old Testament, the second-generation Jews might question the validity of the prohibition of tattooing. There are other passages in the Old Testament that speak of tattooing in rather favorable terms. In the spring of 1898 Paul Haupt, editor of the Polychrome Bible and professor of Semitic languages in Johns Hopkins University, delivered a talk, *Tattooing Among Semites,* before the Baltimore Folklore Society, calling the attention of his audience to the Biblical

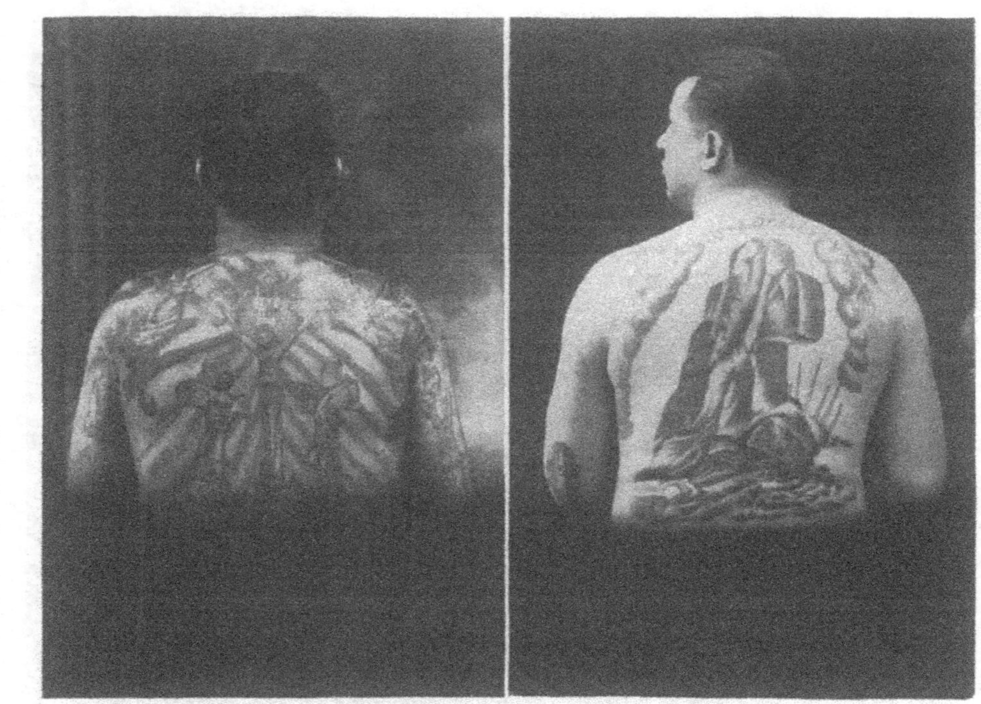

Two of the most universally popular religious tattoos—the Crucified Christ and the Rock of Ages.

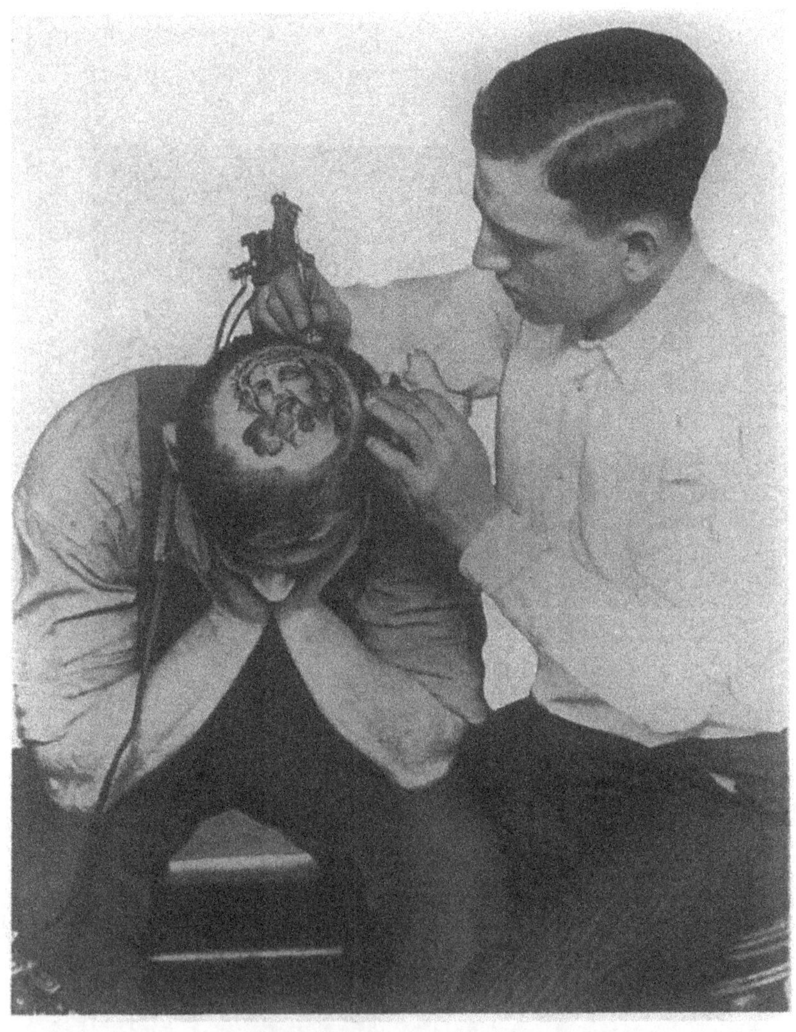

A curiously arresting illustration of the religious motive in tattooing. Bob Wicks is the tattooer, Jack Redcloud the tattooee.

text of Isaiah testifying that "God Himself has engraved the walls of Jerusalem upon the palms of His hands as a pledge that He will restore them." And if any Christians wanted endorsements of tattoo from their own New Testament, Professor Haupt referred them to Galatians and Revelations. This should have dissipated the last doubts of those faithful Christians who as yet adhered to the old Puritanic respect for the Leviticus tattoo-prohibition.

3

In England the late Sutherland Macdonald once revealed that among his clients he had priests, pastors and monks, and that religious designs were almost the only ones chosen by them. He tattooed a serpent around a cross on a bishop's arm; a crucifix nearly one foot long on the chest of a Jesuit missionary bound for China; the badge of a religious order on a community of monks. Frank Howard disclosed that once he tattooed the arm of an American lady-missionary, on the eve of her departure for Korea, with the pictures of horseshoe, anchor and heart inscribed: "Good Luck to All." Louis Morgan, the San Francisco tattooer, wrote in 1912: "A noted missionary had the Ten Commandments inscribed upon his bosom before departing for his mission." In America, says Charlie Wagner, those priests who want to get tattooed go in for general designs in preference to religious symbols. Says he: "They see some picture on the skin of a parishioner and like it. They get in touch with me and ask for a duplicate. But they have it tattooed on a part of the body where it's hidden by the clothes. Also, they wouldn't have it done here in the shop. No, sir, they have it done private."

In none of these cases can we detect unalloyed piety as the only reason for these tattooings. The missionaries hoped to impress their future flocks of superstitious heathens. The monks, in line with their general self-denying, flagellant calling, wanted a fresh mode of self-infliction. Wagner's customers, however subconsciously, wanted to identify themselves with their flocks, wishing to hold those flocks, perhaps feeling that the flocks were being tempted away from their pastors by the secular pastimes of the modern age; the herd-imitation motive, in short, but devoid of its exhibitionist feature.

An American may select a serpent or a tiger or a rose for his arm or chest for no particular reason. But a tattoo-master will take care to explain to him that a serpent is the symbol of both wisdom and eternity, that a tiger represents strength, or that a rose is the magic symbol of love and constancy. Neither the tattooed nor the tattooer is aware of the phallic significance of the serpent's form as the reason for the serpent's role in the general folklore. He is not aware of the totemic role that the tiger played in the dreams of primitive man. He does not know that the erotic, feminine element of the rose lies in its overwhelming fragrance.

But sailors do not need much propaganda from the tattoo-artists. An American sailor relies heavily on a pig, or, now and then, a rooster. A pig, or a pig's head, is generally tattooed on the sailor's left instep. The old-timers consider it a charm against trouble, more particularly a sure charm against the sailor's drowning. Sometimes, a humorous headgear is given the pig, but it does not mean that the sailor is making fun of the superstition. It is a genial belief, this belief in a pig-tattoo on the foot, and the average sailor or tattoo-master does not see why he should be solemn about it. A little fun does not hamper the working of the charm. But I have not as yet seen a single rooster-design with a humorous touch. Is it because the Christian faith finds here its echo? I refer back to the times when American sailors brought from Jerusalem tattooings representing Peter and the crowing cock. Perhaps the modern rooster on the sailor's right foot, guarding him against catastrophes, is the descendant of Peter's rooster, and you couldn't be funny about it. True, in some cases an erotic touch is added to the rooster. In Los Angeles I saw a tattoo-design showing a naked maiden astride a rooster. But there is nothing side-splitting about the scene; it had the crude earnestness of a primitive belief, as if the girl had united with the rooster to save the sailor from a watery grave.

Basically of course the rooster is selected because he is the herald of the dawn, the prophet of awakening, of resurrection. But why the pig, one of the poorest swimmers in the animal kingdom? The tattooers say that the old-time sailors honored the pig because of the salt pork on which they chiefly subsisted during their long ocean voyages.

There may be also an element of defiant charm in the favoring of the pig. The human being will often go against his own beliefs if only for the queer pain-pleasure of daring to invoke the wrath of the gods. The pig is a poor swimmer —let us dare the fates by ordering a tattooed picture of the pig as a charm against drowning. Presently daring becomes a habit. The pig seriously and not ironically becomes the symbol of non-drowning.

Black cats are now often considered good-luck animals instead of the bad-luck bringers that they used to be. It may be that the comic strips, with their genial Felix the Cat, are responsible for this change. At any rate, many tattoo-fans say that they carry black cats on their skin "for good luck," and the Aviators' Club in Los Angeles went so far as to order a tattoo combination of a Black Cat and 13 for each member. Sometimes a black cat is shown emerging from a horseshoe—a double-luck emblem. Two American bathing beauties got themselves photographed for the tabloids with their comely knees tattooed with such defiant charms as a ladder and 13, and an umbrella and 13. Thus the black cat, the ladder, the umbrella, and 13 go the way of the pig.

More self-evident is the origin and the supposed function of such designs and mottoes as follows:

Open eyes are tattooed on American sailors' lids or around their nipples because the sailors believe that such tattoos will keep watch for them when they are tired or asleep.* I am also told of a few cases where a pair of ship's propellers, or twin screws, were tattooed on the sailors' buttocks. The claim is that such designs enhance the dexterity of a man's movement on deck and shore. Some sailors and shore-mechanics go in for hinges tattooed on their arms, on each side of the elbow. This, they say, gives their arms more swing and strength. Some seamen have on their hand-knuckles the magic legend, "Hold Fast," a tattooed letter to each knuckle, thumbs excepting. Others prefer the legend, "True Love," and insist that it is just as lucky as the nautical term, keeping them from falling from aloft.

4

Finally, tattoo as magic is held to be a good instrument not only to bring protection, salvation and general luck, but also to combat disease.

Many Americans and immigrants see medicinal qualities in the very act of tattooing. The Pennsylvania Pole mentioned above was an extreme example of this belief. He was tattooed from head to toe, but he would not tell me the reason. Later Professor Ted told me that this man gets tattooed on a member of his body every time he ails in that particular spot. He claims immediate relief after each tattooing. If there is already a design on the afflicted spot, it is surcharged. The tat-

* Some Americans returning from a sojourn in Japan bring with them pictures of bats tattooed on their bodies. In Japan bats, as nocturnal animals, are tattooed for better eyesight.

tooers of New York estimate that from 1909 to 1933, John Solinsky's tattooings have cost him no less than $10,000. He is employed as a janitor.

Charlie Wagner tells me that some of his aching clients request the work of the tattooing machine without the inks; he claims that rheumatism particularly is helped by electric tattooing, inky or inkless. Billy Donnelly in his Brooklyn days had a customer, an old man, who came regularly to be drilled with the electric needles around his joints, claiming that the vibration and the letting of blood loosened the congestion there and relieved his rheumatics.* British soldiers in India like to assert that the well-tattooed rarely report sick. In 1912 Louis Morgan solemnly proclaimed: "It is well known that a good-sized tattoo is as good an inoculation as any vaccination, and people who have considerable tattoo work on their bodies are generally more healthy than they who have none." A decade later, Professor Jack proclaimed that many American sailors continued, even in the enlightened 1920's, to regard tattooing "as good as vaccination," that any tattoo is "protection against disease."

That such beliefs are considerably older than the electric tattoo-tool may be seen from the fact that among certain tribes of Syria and Egypt tattooing has for centuries been used to "cure" lumbago, sciatica, neuralgia, and other such diseases. A blue spot on each temple, as a preventive of head-

* This belief sometimes merges with the camouflaging purpose of tattooing. Donnelly had another customer who asked him to tattoo his gums red. The man suffered from anemia and said that tattooing would relieve him. Donnelly's guess was that the man knew that tattooing wouldn't help his anemia, that he ordered the operation not for medicinal but for camouflaging ends. He was ashamed of his illness and wanted to conceal it by making the gums artificially and permanently red. The same camouflaging reason prompts bald persons to request the tattooers to prick their bald heads with a semblance of hair. Such cases are fairly numerous. Not long ago Dad Liberty reported that he had tattooed imitation hair on the head of an instructor of the Massachusetts Institute of Technology, who had been burned in a chemical laboratory explosion.

ache, is with many races an old magic tattoo-design. In Burma tattooing is believed to be a charm against any kind of pain; a special "Mooy Say" tattoo is supposed to help against snake bite; it is tattooed on the patient while he holds human flesh between his teeth.

But, far from preventing or curing illnesses, tattoo often is a direct cause of disease. Dr. Marvin D. Shie remarks: "Serious complications are in large measure dependent on the method used and the precautions employed to prevent infection during and after the operation. Formerly it was not uncommon to encounter complications such as gangrene, blood poisoning, and lockjaw, and a number of deaths have occurred as a direct result of tattooing." He mentions that among other diseases, leprosy and tuberculosis have been reported as having been transmitted through the process of tattooing, and that so many syphilis cases have been the result of tattooing "that in some districts the presence of a tattoo is taken as synonymous with a positive Wassermann reaction."

The most notable example of tattooing as a means of communicating syphilis was provided in 1877 by James Kelly, age twenty-six, a Philadelphian, a house-painter by trade, a tattooer and vagrant by preference. The doctors examining him described him as "a man of extremely bad habits, a very hard drinker, a constant chewer of tobacco, and of filthy personal appearance." The most remarkable part of this drama was that this was not his first stay in the Philadelphia Hospital. He had been there three times before, earlier in the year, had been treated for syphilis and while there had tattooed and infected other patients and even a male nurse! It was a wonder that on his three voluntary stays in the hospital (before his arrest in October) he had not extended his tattooing and infecting services to the doctors themselves.

His first visit to the hospital was made on February 17, 1877, with some four or five freshly acquired chancres. He had never had syphilis before. After the treatment he left the hospital (March 6th) and went to Reading and Jersey City where he tattooed and infected a number of men, some of whom were later traced or turned up themselves and treated. On April 14th Kelly returned to Philadelphia and the hospital, and was again treated. He left on May 16, went to Reading again and tattooed some more customers.

On June 20th he again returned, by way of Jersey City, to the Philadelphia Hospital, but was discharged on August 2nd, not for any medical reasons but for insubordination. He went to Jersey City, and returned to Philadelphia on October 6th, while the belated alarm for his apprehension was being sounded. A week later he was arrested and by the end of October the doctors who wished to examine him found him not in the hospital, but in the House of Correction.

The number of men infected by Kelly ran into scores, but only twenty-two cases were included in the study subsequently published by the doctors of the Philadelphia Hospital. The spread of the disease was definitely traced to the man's habit of moistening the color-pigments by putting his needles into his mouth. In his tattoo-work he used India ink, vermilion, coal dust, saliva and water. His fees were anything from a drink of whiskey to two dollars. The figures he made were, to quote his doctors, "often very handsome, and always skilfully done." Most of his victims were in their twenties, four were from sixteen to nineteen, one was thirty-seven. They were mostly general laborers and iron workers, but there were also a male nurse, a coach painter, a japanner, an ice carrier, a brushmaker, a boatman, a wool-washer, a brickmaker, a machinist, a teamster, and a butcher. One young man, of no particular occupation, came of good family and had had no sexual intercourse prior to being tattooed by, and contracting syphilis from Kelly. Most were native-born Americans. A few were Irish.

To this date, only in three American cities, Cleveland, Norfolk and San Francisco, have the authorities prohibited or regulated certain kinds of tattooing. In at least one city, Seattle, the health department sends out inspectors to see that tattooers use aseptic methods and sterilized instruments. In some states, such as New York, the work of tattoo-removal is considered by law to be the proper province of licensed physicians and not tattooers, but from my personal observation I gather that the regulation is enforced very laxly, if at all, especially in New York where tattooers generally do the removal work without any interference from the authorities. Dr. Shie writes that "unfortunate complications of tattooing do not commonly occur today if the operation is done by a modern professional tattooer," for such men usually take all the necessary sanitary precautions, yet "even with them, infections are not rare." But even as early as 1913 Dr. Farenholt said that in not one case out of the 3,575 cases studied by him in the American navy in the period of more than eight years, did he find any evidence of infection, transmission of disease, or blood-poisoning due to tattooing.

It is generally conceded that the electric process, shortening, as it does, the time of tattooing and scaling, diminishes the chances of post-operative complications. The old hand method, clumsy and slow, was responsible for many more cases of gangrene, blood-poisoning and lockjaw.

It is commonly known that latter-day American navy men are somewhat careful. They do not get tattooed in the cold season as much as in warm weather, the general belief among them being that a tattoo done in winter brings on a cold and perhaps pneumonia. There is something to this belief if we consider that the tattooing process lowers, for the time being, the general resistance of the body and thus makes it easier for the man to catch cold in bad weather.

The least harmful consequence of tattooing is the itching

of the skin experienced each spring for many years after. It is confined to those cases where designs were done in vermilion. But the inflammation of the wound after the operation is inevitable whatever the process or colors used. A popular remedy for this inflammation among many tattooers is the application of garlic to the wound.

XI

removal

1

FROM my notebook of cases I pair the following:

1. On January 24, 1923, in Newark, New Jersey, one James Scanlon was arraigned before Police Judge Boettner on a charge of attempted suicide. Scanlon denied that he had wanted to end his life, explaining that on December 18 he had lain down beside a track in the Pennsylvania Railroad yards with his left arm extended over the rail until a passing locomotive amputated it. He had done this because he wanted to get rid of tattoo-decorations on his arm.

2. On the night of December 5, 1924, one Rudolph Sironi, age 19, a violinist, died in a taxicab as he was being taken from Brooklyn Bridge to his home in Manhattan. His hands and wrists were found to be in bandages up to the elbows; in his overcoat pocket was a slip of paper: "Received $150 for removing all ink from both arms. Signed, E. Francisco." Later a relative stated that Sironi had been planning a concert tour and wanted to appear before the public with no tattoo-marks on his hands.

Cases like these two, when reported in the press, help to

strengthen a widespread fallacy, namely that tattoo-inks are indelible. True, if a tattooed man follows some of the old superstitions and tries to eliminate the marks by the use of vinegar, stale urine, mother's milk, garlic, pepper and lime, excrement of pigeons, or other outlandish things, he will not be successful, whether he pricks them into the skin through a needle or spreads them over the designs in ointments. However, I did meet men who showed me faint marks of blue and red tattoos that had been removed, as they claimed, by many periodic injections of cow's milk or heavy cream. Their assertions sounded sincere enough. Andy Sturtz, the Bowery tattooer, is one of the strongest believers in this mode of removal. He explains it by the work of bacteria present in milk. The bacteria are depended upon to destroy the pigment of the tattoos when the milk is injected into the skin.

Along with these beliefs in milk and stranger substances, there persisted for centuries a belief in burning the tattooed design with a red-hot iron. It eliminated the design but usually left an ugly scar instead. A scar of indefinite form was, however, often preferable to a tattoo-mark definitely branding the person a slave or a criminal.

Today we know of better, surer, and less painful methods. In this country, in the early 1890's, Dr. A. H. Ohmann-Dumesnil, professor of dermatology in the St. Louis College of Physicians and Surgeons, successfully removed many tattooed designs from his patients' skin, leaving only faint scars. He used glycerole of papoid which he injected into these designs through fine needles. Unlike the injection of India ink or other tattooing pigments, the injection of the glycerole of papoid produced no swelling or inflammatory reaction. In some cases the tattooing pigments were so strong and so deep-seated that the removal process had to be repeated twice. Dr. Ohmann-Dumesnil claimed that this successful method was, in a degree, originated by the natives of the Indian Archipelago and brought to his attention by a certain Dr. Dupuy. In 1927 Dr. Marvin D. Shie favorably reported a removal method where a fifty percent solution of tannic acid was injected into the tattooed designs, followed, after the sloughing of the skin, by rubbing silver nitrate into the treated area. A yellowed newspaper clipping in Charlie Wagner's possession, of no definite date or origin, states that this tannin-nitrate method of removal has also been used by "Parisian beauty doctors" operating among tattooed society people.

Another method is electrolytic. It is used to eliminate very small designs, such as miniature butterflies, tiny monograms, etc. Still another method is that of surgery. It is to cut off the skin, including the objectionable design and to graft new skin on, under chloroform. In 1917 Arthur Randolph Martin, a circus man of West Virginia, came to a Baltimore hospital to have this method used on him in getting rid of Kaiser Wilhelm's portrait tattooed on his chest. I also hear that a certain French doctor resorts to this method and at the same time gathers samples of tattooed skin for his unique collection.

The tattoo-masters of New York and other American cities use various chemical solutions in their removal work. They shoot these fluids into the designs on the skin through their regular tattooing needles, repeating the tattooing process in the reverse. In New York, as in a few other cities, the removal work being under the theoretical surveillance of the proper health authorities, the tattooers claim, some honestly and some not, that their chemicals are procured from reliable doctors or chemists. Charlie Wagner says that he received his from a Fordham University student of medicine. The student had been tattooed in his early youth. Shortly before graduation he grew concerned over the possible effect of red-and-blue hands on his patients. He busied himself in the University laboratory with various fluids, and the result of his experiments was an acid which he brought to Wagner. "Try it on me," he said to Wagner. It was a complete success, and the jubilant student presented Wagner with the formula as payment. Sailor Joe Van Hart uses a white substance which he thinks is powdered magnesia. He gets it from Sidney Wright, a Philadelphia tattooer who experiments in removal pigments. However, this white substance removes designs for a limited period of time only; the tattoo reappears after a year or so. Louis Morgan, the San Francisco tattooer, may have used the same substance when, writing in 1912, he described a "Chinese white paint in powder form" as a good removing agent if mixed with a very weak carbolic acid. However, to be safe, he cautioned not to "work over a spot larger than a dime in one place."

Other removal methods recommended in Morgan's curious manual are: 1) four parts of slacked lime to one part sulphur, mixed together dry and supplemented with a small percentage of powdered phosphorus, wetted with water, applied to the tattoo immediately after wetting the mixture; 2) nitric acid, to be applied to the skin for periods of two to three minutes, and then washed off with clear cold water; 3) three parts of chloride of zinc to four parts of sterilized water; 4) zinc mixed with salt.

The methods of tattoo removal scientifically tested and approved by chemists, physicians and surgeons are as follows:

1. French process—tannic acid and silver nitrate.
2. Salicylic acid.
3. Monochloracetic or trichloracetic acid.
4. Carbolic acid (Phenol).
5. Sulphuric acid (15 grains to 1 oz of H_2O/water/).
6. Nitric acid (concentrated).
7. Zinc chloride.
8. Mercuric chloride.
9. Cantharides plaster (Spanish fly). Add vinegar to increase its action.

Or: Open the blister formed by Spanish fly and add a weak zinc chloride solution.

10. Glycerole of papoid (or glycerole of caroid). A powerful organic digestant; it digests the tissue in question.
11. Zonite, a solution of sodium hypochlorite, approximately twice as strong as Dakin's solution.
12. Electrolysis—similar to hair-removal by electricity; feasible only on small tattoo-designs.
13. Surgery: cut mechanically, raise the flap of the cut skin, scrape off the pigment from the bottom of the skin.
14. Surgery: use a grattage (a little steel scrubbing brush), apply hydrogen peroxide.
15. Use cutaneous trephine (a surgical instrument resembling a hollow carpenter's tool).
16. When a design is superficial, use dry ice (CO_2 snow). It will freeze the skin, turning it gray; then the skin may be removed with tweezers.
17. For long thin designs: simple excision.
18. For larger designs: excision with skin grafting.

These methods are not to be used by the tattooed themselves or by tattoo masters but by physicians or surgeons only. The list is compiled on the basis of chemical and medical literature dealing with tattooing and its removal.

Most of the tattoo-masters say that the process of removal takes from ten days to two weeks, that in larger designs it takes longer, that there is no soreness either during or after the process, and that the removal results in a reddish surface which soon becomes smooth and of natural color. There is no doubt that they are overconfident as to this smoothness and naturalness. Dr. Shie states that none of the removal methods is perfect, that "all of them leave a scar of greater or less degree, but the resultant scar in any case should be no more marked than that of a superficial burn and often is so slight that close scrutiny is required to detect it." He describes the quack methods of some tattoo practitioners in their removal work, and strongly advises that those wishing to have their tattoos removed apply to good physicians and not to the tattoo-masters.

Of course there are no two removal operations alike in their result. Much depends on the skin of the patient in question. Frank Howard used to say that some skins are "as delicately thin as a rose leaf," while others are "as stout as a buck-skin glove." Naturally, it is much harder to operate on a rose-leaf skin than on a buck-skin, both when tattooing and when removing. Again, the old hand-needles went into the skin deeper than the modern electric needles; the old work, consequently, is more permanent and is harder to remove. Also, much depends on whether the tattooer was known for his light touch or cursed for his heavy hand. A light-touch design is easier to take off than the heavy-hand splash.

Again, what pigments were used by the original tattooer? Vermilion, for instance, will naturally fade or disappear much more easily than gunpowder or India ink. Indigo may also become very dim after a lapse of years and thus be easily eradicated by the remover. But the India inks will last in their original vividness for twenty and thirty years, practically a lifetime. The old idea was that the India ink went into *flesh* too deep to be taken out by any methods or chemicals. In 1890 a writer recalled in the Boston *Commercial Bulletin*:

> At Mount Washington University Hospital, Baltimore, an experiment was some years ago made upon the forearm of a noted character of that city who died there. One of the students, curious to learn everything possible connected with the practice of tattooing, cut from the dead man's arm a strip of skin upon which a coat of arms appeared. Beneath the skin the design remained visible. By degrees the flesh was removed, the design in India ink still remaining in sight until finally the bone was reached.

> After a thorough sponging for the purpose of removing the blood and pieces of flesh remaining it was found that the representation still appeared. After cutting away a small section of the bone the India ink mark was found not to have penetrated beyond.

But the real reason for the permanency of the India ink is not the depth to which it penetrates but its peculiar chemical composition defying all attempts to dissolve it and thus eliminate the tattoo even when an India ink tattoo does not happen to penetrate deeply.

Finally, how much is there to remove? A small design is easier to remove than large pictures occupying an entire back or a whole chest. If the operation leaves a scar—and it often does—a small design would leave a small scar, causing little pain during the process of removal, but a large design would leave a terrible life-time deformation.

2

Tattoo-masters tell me that they never ask a man why he wants his designs removed. The customers may be navy or army men who have deserted and now want to eliminate these means of identification. They may be civilian criminals trying to escape detection. On the other hand, they are often men of honorable intentions, now in their prime and ashamed of their youthful tattoo-marks, especially if they are risqué. They may wish to get married, and the ladies of their choice may object to the tattoo-marks. In Los Angeles there was the case of a young man who secured a job at a soda fountain on condition that he have the tattoo-designs removed from his arms. The proprietor said that his customers might be rather fidgety about being served by tattooed hands. James Scanlon, of the Newark case cited at the opening of

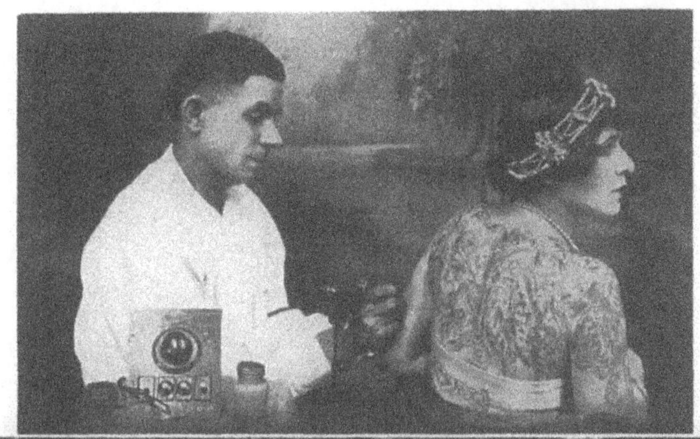

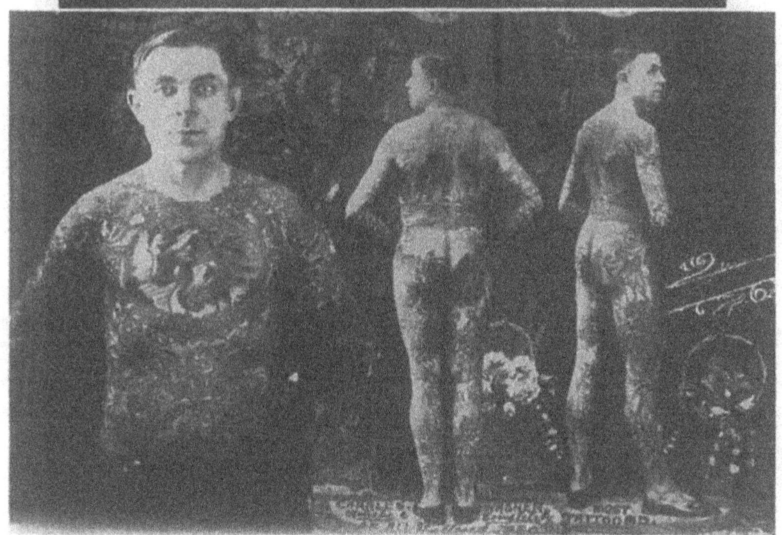

Some intimate views of Professor Charles Wagner as tattoo-ist and tattooee.

this chapter, declared to the judge that he had his arm cut off because he "got tired" looking at the tattoos.

After America's entrance into the World War many Americans tried to get rid of tattoo-designs of a nature suddenly become unpatriotic. Besides the circus performer who had Kaiser Wilhelm's portrait on his chest, there were thousands of American seamen with flags-of-all-nations designs on their bodies, and among other flags was, of course, the German flag, now a stigma to be removed.

Obscene designs and pictures of nude women are often removed because they have been officially frowned upon in the American navy since 1909. However, to comply with this prohibition, the extreme method—that of removal—is not obligatory. It is enough for a sailor to order a bathing suit tattooed on the figure. Other more complicated or more obscene designs are censored in various ingenious ways. Generally the surcharge of one design upon another is resorted to rather than removal. It causes less pain and does not endanger health and life. It takes less time—a valuable consideration with deserters and criminals trying to make their getaway. Also, removal costs about four times as much as surcharge.

But the surchargers must know their designs and colors. They must know that birds of rich plumage and willow-trees of luxuriant growth are the best designs to cover other designs grown objectionable. They must remember that a black design will eventually show through a red surcharge; that any India ink will show through vermilion or an indigo surcharge; that a crude gunpowder tattoo, being full of indissoluble carbon and therefore very black, will peep through the most skilful surcharge done in vermilion or indigo; and that a black tint is generally a sure coverer of all other tattoo-sins of other shades.

3

In the man's desire to remove the tattoo marks two forces usually combine: outside pressure and an inner change. As in acquiring the tattoo, so in the removal, the man feels an urge to subject himself to the operation for deep-seated reasons of his own, but often it takes a push from the outside for him to voice this inner change and go through with the operation.

Masochism—the desire to experience the pain of tattooing—plays its role in the original process of acquiring pictures. So it does in the process of removal, only now the pain is subconsciously in retribution for the original tattoo-sin. The outside pressure of some particularly attractive design plays its role in the acquiring of a tattoo. Gradually grown conventional to the wearer's taste it loses its original appeal, it becomes as objectionable as it used to be attractive. The outside pressure of its ugliness now so evident compels him to have it removed. Or, the outside pressure of a friend tattoo-addict in the first case is matched by subsequent pressure of another friend or relative opposed to tattooing generally or to this particular design. Again, the outside pressure of the herd-imitation motive—the pressure that helped the man to voice some inner need for tattooing—is now opposed and nullified by a new herd with which the tattoo-wearer falls in, a herd frowning upon the tattoo and thus striking some newer anti-tattoo chord in the man's subconscious.

The guilt complex that drives a man to get tattooed as a self-inflicted punishment for his vague sin inferiority feelings repeats its work in the reversal some years later. The man now experiences the same guilt feeling but attaches it to the very fact of his wearing these peculiar decorations.

The martyr complex that drives the man to undergo the pain of tattooing will reassert itself in his desire to represent himself as a victim of circumstances. He will gradually begin to blame for his tattooing a wild impulse, a drunken spell, the influence of a war-period or a navy-environment or a wicked comrade. He will exhibit his tattoos to all who will look and listen. He will call for their denunciation of the tattoo-art and for their pity. He will assure his onlookers and listeners that he would pay anything to have his tattoos removed. Tell him that nowadays one can safely have tattoos removed, and he will become uneasy rather than delighted.

For his pleasure is not in removal but in his self-pitying, self-glorifying talk of removal. If he does have his designs removed he will sneak into a tattooer's shop at some later date to order fresh designs, that he may have a renewed opportunity to blame an impulse, a drunken spell, a bad chum, that he may call once more for pity of his fellow-men, to relive in imagination and talk the old pain-pleasure of the operation, be it the acquirement of a tattoo or its removal.

bibliography

English

ANONYMOUS, Branding and Tattooing. *Every Saturday,* BOSTON, FEBRUARY 21, 1874.

Human Documents. *Good Words,* LONDON, NOVEMBER, 1905. Illustrated.

Japanese Tattooing. *Nature,* LONDON AND NEW YORK, OCTOBER 8, 1885.

Tattooing is Not So Common In Our New Navy. *Literary Digest,* NEW YORK, SEPTEMBER 6, 1919.

Prosperity Flourishes Unchecked in the Tattoo Industry. *Literary Digest,* NEW YORK, OCTOBER 1, 1932.

ASHTON-WOLFE, H., Tattooing and the Criminal. *Illustrated London News,* AUGUST 11, 1928.

The Forgotten Clue. Stories of the Parisian Sûreté With an Account of its Methods. BOSTON AND NEW YORK: Houghton Mifflin Company, 1930. See: Tattooing and the Criminal, second division in Chapter IX (practically the same material as in his article in the *Illustrated London News*).

BARTON, F. R., Tattooing in South Eastern New Guinea. *Journal of the Royal Anthropological Institute of Great Britain and Ireland,* LONDON, 1918, v.48. Illustrated.

BEST, ELSDON, The Uhi-Maori, or Native Tattooing Instruments. *Journal of the Polynesian Society,* WELLINGTON, N. Z., 1904, V.13.

BOLTON, GAMBIER, Pictures on the Human Skin. *Strand Magazine,* LONDON, APRIL, 1897. Illustrated.

BOYLE, V., The Marking of Girls at Ga-Anda. *African Soc. Journal,* LONDON, 1916, V.15.

BUCKLAND, A. W. (MISS), On Tattooing. *Journal of the Anthropological Institute of Great Britain and Ireland,* LONDON, MAY, 1888, V.17.

COWAN, JAMES, Maori Tattooing Survivals. Some Notes on Moco. *Journal of the Polynesian Society,* NEW PLYMOUTH, N. Z., 1921, V.30. Illustrated.

CUNNINGHAM, CHARLES, Tattooing Among the Early Maoris. *Empire Review,* LONDON, FEBRUARY, 1932.

DAVIES, G. H., The Origin of Tattooing. *Journal of the Polynesian Society,* NEW PLYMOUTH, N. Z., 1911. V.20.

DEL MAR, F., Year Among the Maoris. *Discovery,* LONDON, OCTOBER, 1924. Illustrated.

DRACOTT, C. H., Tatuing in India and Amongst the Aborigines. *Reliquary and Illus. Archael.,* LONDON, 1908, V.14.

DURHAM, MARY EDITH, Some Tribal Origins, Laws and Customs of the Balkans. Illustrated by the author. LONDON: G. Allen & Unwin, Ltd., 1928. See pp. 101-103 (tattooing and the symbols tattooed).

ELLIS, HAVELOCK, The Criminal. 5th edition, revised and enlarged. LONDON: the Walter Scott Publishing Co., 1914. See pp. 191-201.

FARENHOLT, A., DR., Some Statistical Observations Concerning Tattooing as Seen by a Recruiting Surgeon. *U. S. Naval Medical Bulletin,* WASHINGTON, D.C., JANUARY, 1913, V.7, no. 1 (quoted at length in the New York Sunday *Times,* June 8, 1913, Magazine Section).

FISHBEIN, MORRIS, DR., The Removal of Tattooing. *Scientific American,* NEW YORK, APRIL, 1928.

FLAHERTY, F. H., Fa'a-Samoa. *Asia,* NEW YORK, DECEMBER, 1925.

FLETCHER, ROBERT, Tattooing Among Civilized People. Read before the Anthropological Society of Washington, December 19, 1882. WASHINGTON, D. C.: Judd & Deitweiler, 1883.

FRANKS, A. W., Tattooed Man from Burmah. *Journal of the Anthropological Institute of Great Britain and Ireland,* LONDON, 1873, V.2.

GASCOIGNE, G. E., DR., A Letter on Chambers, the Tattooed Canadian. *Lancet,* LONDON, MAY 18, 1872.

GEARE, RANDOLPH I., How Savages Ornament Their Bodies. *Out West,* LOS ANGELES, CAL., SEPTEMBER, 1909.

Tattooing. *Scientific American,* NEW YORK, SEPTEMBER 12, 1903.

GORDON, MARY LOUISA, Penal Discipline. LONDON: G. Routledge & Sons, Ltd.; NEW YORK: E. P. Dutton & Co., 1922. See pp. 129-143 on the tattooed woman.

GUPTE, B. A., Notes on Female Tattoo Designs in India. *Indian Antiquary,* BOMBAY, 1902, V.31.

HADDON, ERNEST B., The Dog-motive in Bornean Art. *Journal of the Anthropological Institute of Great Britain and Ireland,* LONDON, 1905, V.35.

HAMBLY, W. D., Ancient and Modern Tattooing. *Nautical Magazine,* GLASGOW AND LONDON, MAY, 1921.

The History of Tattooing and Its Significance. LONDON: H. F. & G. Witherby, publishers, 1925 (published in the United States in 1927 by The Macmillan Company).

The Significance of Corporal Marking. *Hibbert Journal,* LONDON, JANUARY, 1926, V.24.

HANDY, EDWARD SMITH CRAIGHILL, AND HANDY, WILLOWDEAN C., Samoan House Building, Cooking and Tattooing. HONOLULU: The Museum, 1924.

HANDY, WILLOWDEAN C. (MRS.), Tattooing in the Marquesas. HONOLULU: The Museum, 1922 (includes bibliography).

Where Beauty Is Skin Deep. Tattooing of the Marquesans, an Indigenous Development Now Fading Under Influence of Civilization. *International Studio,* NEW YORK, MARCH, 1923. Illustrated.

HILER, HILAIRE, From Nudity to Raiment; an introduction to the study of costume. NEW YORK: F. Weyhe, 1929. See pp. 83-91.

bibliography

HOPKINS, TIGHE, The Art and Mystery of Tattooing. *Leisure Hour,* LONDON, 1895, V.44, pp. 694-698, 774-780. Illustrated.

HOSE, CHARLES, AND SHELFORD, R., Materials for a Study of Tatu in Borneo. *Journal of the Anthropological Institute of Great Britain and Ireland,* LONDON, 1906, V.36.

HOWARD, FRANK (interview with), The Gentle Art of Tattooing. *Westminster Budget,* JANUARY 7, 1898.

HUNT, DANIEL, AND HUMPHREYS, LINCOLN, Samoan Tattooing. *U. S. Naval Medical Bulletin,* WASHINGTON, D. C., MARCH, 1923, V.18.

KUPER, HENRY, Tapitapi, or The Tattooing of Females on Santa Anna and Santa Catalina (Solomon Group). *Journal of the Polynesian Society,* NEW PLYMOUTH, N. Z., 1926, V.35.

LOMBROSO, CESARE, PROF., The Savage Origin of Tattooing. *Popular Science Monthly,* NEW YORK, APRIL, 1896. Illustrated.

LUARD, C. E., Tattooing in Central India. *Indian Antiquary,* BOMBAY, 1904, V.33.

MALLERY, GARRICK, Picture-Writing of the American Indians. Published by the Smithsonian Institution, Bureau of Ethnology, WASHINGTON, D. C., 1894 (contains a chapter on tattooing. Illustrated).

MAURY, F. F., AND DULLES, C. W., DRS., Tattooing as a Means of Communicating Syphilis. *American Journal of the Medical Sciences,* PHILADELPHIA, JANUARY, 1878.

MELL, C. D., Tattooing Dyes from Fruits of Randia. *Textile Colorist,* NEW YORK, JUNE, 1926, V.48.

MINNEGERODE, FITZHUGH LEE, "Tattooing" in Mayfair. New York Sunday *Times,* MARCH 14, 1926.

MORGAN, LOUIS (tattooer). The Modern Tattooist. BERKELEY, CAL.: The Courier Publishing Company, 1912. Illustraded (brochure).

MURPHY, JAY, Their Beauty Is Only Skin Deep. *Everybody's,* NEW YORK, OCTOBER, 1926. Illustrated.

MURRAY, F. E., The Tattoo Method of Marking Hogs and Its Use. U. S. Department of Agriculture, Miscellaneous Circular

No. 57, issued March, 1926, revised February, 1929. WASHINGTON, D. C. Illustrated.

MYERS, CHARLES E., Contributions to Egyptian Anthropology: Tatuing. *Journal of the Anthropological Institute of Great Britain and Ireland,* LONDON, 1903, V.33.

NAKANO, SUYEO, Tattooing in Japan. *Trans-Pacific,* TOKYO, APRIL 24, 1930.

O'BRIEN, FREDERICK, Atolls of the Sun. NEW YORK: The Century Company, 1922 (see Chapter XVII).

OHMANN-DUMESNIL, A. H., DR., Tattooing and Its Successful Removal. *New York Medical Journal,* MAY 20, 1893.

O'REILLY, SAMUEL F. (tattooer), The Art of Tattooing in Ancient and Modern Times. All About Tattooing and How It is Done in Various Parts of the World. Published by the author, NEW YORK, 1900 (brochure).

PARRY, ALBERT, The Tattoo Crisis. *Haldeman-Julius Quarterly,* GIRARD, KANSAS, APRIL, 1928 (reprinted in Stories of Tramp Life, Little Blue Book no. 1412, Girard, Kansas, 1929).

The Depression in Chatham Square. *New Yorker,* DECEMBER 24, 1932 (see A Reporter at Large).

Magic in American Tattooing. *American Mercury,* NEW YORK, MAY, 1933.

RICH, LOUIS, Tattooing Enters On Machine Age. New York Sunday *Times,* SEPTEMBER 14, 1930.

ROBLEY, HORATIO GORDON, Moko, or Maori Tattooing. LONDON: Chapman & Hall, 1896.

ROTH, H. LING, Artificial Skin Marking in the Sandwich Islands. In *Internationales Archiv für Ethnographie,* LEIDEN, HOLLAND, 1900, V.13. Illustrated.

Maori Tatu and Moko. *Journal of the Anthropological Institute of Great Britain and Ireland,* LONDON, 1901, V.31

Tatu in the Society Islands. *Journal of the Anthropological Institute of Great Britain and Ireland,* LONDON, 1906, V.35.

SAHAI, GANGA, Female Tattooing Amongst Ghilzais. *Indian Antiquary,* BOMBAY, 1904, V.33.

bibliography

SALWEY, CHARLOTTE M., Tattooing (in Japan). *Imperial and Asiatic Quarterly Review,* WOKING, ENGLAND, 1896, series 3, V.2.

SHIE, MARVIN D., DR., Tattooing and Tattoo Removal. *Hygeia,* CHICAGO, DECEMBER, 1927.

A Study of Tattooing and Method of Its Removal. *Journal of the American Medical Association,* CHICAGO, JANUARY 14, 1928.

SINCLAIR, A. T., Tattooing—Oriental and Gypsy. *American Anthropologist,* LANCASTER, PA., JULY-SEPTEMBER, 1908.

Tattooing of the American Indians. *American Anthropologist,* LANCASTER, PA., JULY-SEPTEMBER, 1909.

SMEATON, OLIPHANT, Tattooing and Its History. *Westminster Review,* LONDON, MARCH, 1898.

TEIT, J. A., Tattooing and Face and Body Painting of Thompson Indians of British Columbia. Edited by Franz Boas. WASHINGTON, D. C. 45th report of the Ethnology Bureau, 1927-28, pp. 397-439 (reprinted as a separate bulletin in 1930).

THURSTON, EDGAR, Note on Tattooing. Madras Gov. Museum Bulletin, MADRAS, 1898, V.2, no. 2.

WINKLER, JOHN K., When Art Is a Skin Game (interview with Charlie Wagner). *Collier's,* NEW YORK, FEBRUARY 13, 1926.

The following is a partial list of fiction (in English) in which the tattooing motif figures prominently:

ANDREWS, MARY, The Tattoo. A short story. *Hampton's Magazine,* MARCH, 1909.

CHILD, RICHARD WASHBURN, The Tattoo. A short story. *Collier's,* NEW YORK, NOVEMBER 23, 1912.

CHILTON, JOHN, The Tattooed Leg. A short story. *Overland Monthly,* SAN FRANCISCO, NOVEMBER, 1919.

FORD, COREY, One for All. A humorous short story. *Liberty,* NEW YORK, JUNE 25, 1932.

HAGGARD, HENRY RIDER, SIR, Mr. Meeson's Will. A novel. NEW YORK: Harper & Bros., 1888.

KURASHIGE, TETSU, The Tattooed Man. A short story. *Overland Monthly,* SAN FRANCISCO, MAY, 1919.

OLD SPICER, pseud., The Tattooed Wrist; or The Deed of a Night. NEW YORK: Street & Smith, 1896 (Magnet Detective Library, no. 327).

OSTRANDER, ISABEL E., The Tattooed Arm. A mystery novel. NEW YORK: R. M. McBride & Company, 1922, and A. L. Burt Co., 1924.

VAN VECHTEN, CARL, The Tattooed Countess; a Romantic Novel with a Happy Ending. NEW YORK: Alfred A. Knopf, 1924.

WARD, C., Tattooed Countess, parody. *Saturday Review of Literature,* NEW YORK, FEBRUARY 28, 1925.

For briefer mentions of tattoo also see Van Vechten's "Peter Whiffle" (1922) and "Blind Bow-Boy" (1923), also Mark Twain's "Huckleberry Finn" (Chapter XXIX, "I Light Out in the Storm"). Separately are to be listed Herman Melville's books:

Typee: Narrative of a Four Months' Residence among the Natives of a Valley of the Marquesas Islands. 1846.

Omoo, a Narrative of Adventures in the South Seas. 1847.

Mardi, and a Voyage Thither. 1848.

Redburn, His First Voyage. 1848.

The Whale (or, Moby Dick). 1851.

Herman Melville was the first American writer to acquaint the general reader with the exotic isles and customs of the South Seas, and incidentally with the curious tattooage of the locality. His works are full of references, both fleeting and minute, to the skin-ornaments of the natives. As in regard to other things, fact is freely mixed with fancy in Melville's narrative of tattooing. His tattooed heroes and villains may have existed in the reality of the 1840's, and may not.

Arabic

HILWANI, AHMAD IBN AHMAD IBN ISMAIL AL, A treatise on tattooing. CAIRO, 1880 (a copy is in the Schiff collection of the New York Public Library).

Dutch

KRUYT, J., Het ma'boea en de tatouage in Seka (Midden-Celebes). In *Bijdragen tot de Taal-, Land- en Volkenkunde van Nederlandsch-Indië,* 1920, v.76.

WETERING, F. H. VAN DE, Het tatoueeren op rote. In *Bijdragen tot de Taal-, Land- en Volkenkunde van Nederlandsch-Indië,* 1924, v.80.

French

BAILLOT, Du détatouage. PARIS, 1893-94.

BEJOT, Étude sur le tatouage en Algérie. Soc. d'anthropologie de Paris, Bull. et mémoires, PARIS, 1920.

BERCHON, ERNEST, Un cas de mort dû au tatouage. Union médicale de la Gironde, 1862.

Histoire médicale du tatouage. PARIS, 1869.

BERTHOLON, LUCIEN, Origines néolitiques et mycéniennes des tatouages des indigènes du nord de l'Afrique. *Archives d'anthropologie crim.,* PARIS, 1904, v.19.

BOIGEY, MAURICE, Les détenus tatoués; leur psychologie. *Archives d'anthropologie criminelle,* LYON, 1910. Illustrated.

BONNEMAISON, Tatouage chez les aliénés. PARIS, 1894-95.

BOYER, JACQUES, L'art dans le tatouage. *Le monde moderne,* PARIS, 1902, V. 16.

Le tatouage artistique dans les diverses parties du monde. *La nature,* PARIS, 1898.

CALOYANNI, M., Étude des tatouages sur les criminels d'Égypte. *Institut d'Égypte. Bull. Le Caire,* 1923. Tome 5.

COMTE, J., Tatouage et chirurgie d'armée. PARIS, 1880.

CONVERSET, Tatouage et syphilis. LYON, 1888.

DAGUILLON, Le tatouage chez les aliénés. *Archives d'anthropologie criminelle,* PARIS, 1895.

DÉCHELETTE, JOSEPH, Le peinture corporelle et le tatouage. *Rev. archéol.,* PARIS, 1907, ser.4, v.9.

DECORSE, J., Le tatouage. Les mutilations ethniques et la parure chez les populations du Soudan. *L'Anthropologie,* PARIS, 1905, v.16.

DESCHAMPS, Mémoires sur les cicatrices colorées et incolores des races humaines. Union Médicale, 1861.

GAILLARD, Étude sur les lacustres du Bas-Dahomey. *L'Anthropologie,* PARIS, 1907, v.18.

GEILL, CHRISTIAN, Identification par le tatouage. *Archives d'anthropologie criminelle,* PARIS, 1902.

GOBERT, E., Notes sur les tatouages des indigènes tunisiens. *L'Anthropologie,* PARIS, 1924, v.34. Illustrated.

HERBER, J., Tatouages marocains. Tatouage et religion. *Revue de l'histoire des religions,* PARIS, 1921.

Tatouages des prisonniers marocains (Arabes, Arabisés et Berbères). Hespéris, PARIS, 1925, v.5. Illustrated.

Origine et signification des tatouages marocains. *L'Anthropologie,* PARIS, 1927, v.37.

Tatouages curatifs au Maroc. *Revue d'ethnographie et des traditions populaires,* PARIS, 1929.

Les tatouages nord-africaines sont-ils bleus ou verts? *Revue africaine,* ALGER, 1931, v.72.

HUCHERY, Les mutilations ethniques chez quelques tribus de la région du Moyen-Niger. Institut français d'anthropologie. Comptes rendus des séances. PARIS, 1914, v.2.

HUTIN, Recherches sur le tatouage. *Bul. Acad. méd.,* PARIS, 1853.

JACQUOT, LUCIEN, Étude sur les tatouages des indigènes de l'Algérie. *L'Anthropologie,* PARIS, 1899, v.10.

JOUAN, Cas de mort, suite du tatouage. *Revue coloniale,* APRIL, 1858.

LACASSAGNE, ALEXANDRE, DR., Les tatouages. Étude anthropologique et médico-légale. PARIS, 1881.

Sur le tatouage. Société méd. lég. de France. Bulletin. PARIS, 1881-82.

La signification des tatouages chez les peuples primitifs. Institut de France. Acad. des sciences et politiques. Séances at travaux. PARIS, 1912, v.178, pp. 171-184.

LÉALE, HENRI, Criminalité et tatouage. *Archives d'anthropologie criminelle,* LYON, 1909, v.24.

LOCARD, EDMOND, Le tatouage chez les Hébreux. *Archives d'anthropologie criminelle,* PARIS, 1909, v.24.

LOMBROSO, CESARE, PROF., L'homme criminel. PARIS, 1887 (see pp. 257-289).

MARANDON DE MONTYEL, E., DR., Contribution à l'étude clinique des tatouages chez les aliénés. Documents de criminologie et de médecine légale, LYON: A. Storck, 188–?

Les tatouages chez les aliénés. *Arch. anth. crim.,* PARIS, 1893.

MARCY, G., Origine et signification des tatouages de tribus berbères. *Revue de l'histoire des religions,* PARIS, JULY-DECEMBER, 1930, V.102. Illustrated.

MARTIN, ETIENNE, Le tatouage chez les enfants. *Archives d'anthropol. criminelle,* LYON, 1910, V.25. Illustrated.

MARTIN, PAUL-EUGÈNE, DR., Du tatouage et du détatouage: leur rapport avec l'aliénation mentale. PARIS: Vigot Freres, 1900.

MASSELON, Du tatouage des moignons oculaires. *Ann. d'oculist,* DECEMBER, 1899.

MOTTE-CAPRON, A. MAITROT DE LA, Essai sur les tatouages nord-africains. Soc. de géographie d'Alger et de l'Afrique du Nord. Bull. PARIS, 1927. Illustrated.

NOEL, P., Tatouages et leur technique au Cameron central. *Revue d'ethnographie,* PARIS, 1922. Illustrated.

PERDRIZET, PAUL, La miraculeuse histoire de Pandare et d'Eschédore, suivie de recherches sur la marque dans l'antiquite. *Archiv. für Religionswissenschaft,* LEIPZIG, 1911, V.14.

PLAS, J. VAN DEN, L'opération du tatouage chez les Mobali. *Revue congolaise,* UCCLE, 1910.

SPENAR, H., Du tatouage des Esquimaux. *Bull. société anthropol.,* 1879, p. 590.

TARRAL, Tumeurs érectiles traitées par le tatouage. *Arch. médecine,* 1834.

VERVAECK, LOUIS, Le tatouage en Belgique. Communication faite à la Société d'Anthropologie de Bruxelles. BRUXELLES: Hayez, 1906 (239 pages).

Le tatouage en Belgique. *Archives d'anthropologie criminelle,* LYON, 1907, V.22 (29 pages).

Le tatouage en Belgique. Soc. d'anthropologie de Bruxelles. Bull. et mém., BRUXELLES, 1908, V.25, no. 2 (43 pages).

VIDAL, EDMOND, Les tatouages des Nègres du Congo français. *Rev. européenne,* PARIS, 1912.

German

ELLER, FRITZ, Ein Vorlagebuch für Tätowierungen. *Archiv f. Kriminal-Anthropologie u. Kriminalistik,* LEIPZIG, 1905, V.19. Illustrated.

GLÜCK, LEOPOLD, Die Tätowierung der Haut bei den Katholiken Bosniens und der Hercegovina. *Wissenschaftl. Mittheil. aus Bosnien und der Hercegovina* (Bosnisch-Hercegovinisches Landesmuseum in Sarajevo), VIENNA, 1894, v.2. Illustrated.

HEIN, WILHELM, Zur Tätowierung der Samoaner. *Mittheil. d. K. K. Geograph. Gesellschaft in Wien,* VIENNA, 1899, v.42.

JAEGER, J., Tätowierungen von 150 Verbrechern mit Personalangaben. *Archiv f. Kriminal-Anthropologie,* LEIPZIG, 1905, v.18, v.21.

JOEST, WILHELM, Tätowiren, Narbenzeichnen und Korperbemalen. BERLIN, A. Asher & Co., 1887.

KARUTZ, RICHARD, Tatauiermuster aus Tunis. *Archiv f. Anthropologie,* BRAUNSCHWEIG, 1908, v.35.

KOHLBACH, BERTHOLD, Spuren der Tätowierung im Judentum. *Globus,* BRAUNSCHWEIG, 1910, v.97.

KRÄMER, AUGUSTIN, Die Ornamentik der Kleidmatten und der Tatauierung auf den Marshallinseln nebst technologischen, philologischen und ethnologischen Notizen. *Archiv f. Anthropologie,* BRAUNSCHWEIG, 1904, v.30. Illustrated.

Zur Tatauierung der Mentawei-Insulaner. *Archiv f. Anthropologie,* BRAUNSCHWEIG, 1907, v.34. Illustrated.

Tätowiren, tatauiren, tatuiren, und die wasserflasche. *Internationales Archiv für Ethnographie,* LEIDEN, 1927, v.28.

LASSALLY, OSWALD, Amulette und Tätowierungen in Ägypten. *Archiv für Religionswissenschaft,* LEIPZIG, 1931, v.29.

LAUFFER, OTTO, Ueber die Geschichte und den heutigen volkstümlichen Gebrauch der Tätowierung in Deutschland. *Wörter und Sachen,* HEIDELBERG, 1914, v.6.

MARQUARDT, CARL, Die tätowirung beider Geschlechter in Samoa. BERLIN: D. Reimer, 1899.

MASCHKA, K., Zur Tätowirungsfrage. *Archiv f. Kriminal-Anthropologie u. Kriminalistik,* LEIPZIG, 1899, v.1.

MOHL, JOSEF, Mitteilungen über Tätowierungen, aufgenommen

an Soldaten der Garnison Temesvár. *Anthrop. Gesellsch. Mitteil.,* VIENNA, 1908, v.38.

PARKINSON, R., Tätowierung der Mogemokinsulaner. *Globus,* BRAUNSCHWEIG, 1904, v.86.

RIECKE, ERHARD, Das tatauierungswesen im heutigen Europa. JENA: G. Fischer, 1925. Illustrated.

SENFFT, ARNO, Über die Tätowierung der Westmikronesier. *Globus,* BRAUNSCHWEIG, 1905, v.87.

STEINEN, KARL VON DEN, Die Marquesaner und ihre Kunst; Studien über die Entwicklung primitiver Südseeornamentik nach eigenen Reiseergebnissen und dem Material der Museen. BERLIN: D. Reimer, 1925-28 (three volumes).

STOLPE, HJALMAR, Über die Taetowirung der Oster-Insulaner. *Koenigl. zool. u. anthropologisch-ethnographisches Museum zu Dresden, Abhandlungen u. Berichte,* BERLIN, 1899.

THILENIUS, G., Die Tätowierung der Frauen auf den Laughlaninseln. *Globus,* BRAUNSCHWEIG, 1902, v.81.

TRAEGER, PAUL, Das Handwerkzeug eines tunesischen Tätowierers. *Ztsch. f. Ethnologie,* BERLIN, 1904, v.36. Illustrated.

TRUHELKA, CIRO, Die Tätowirung bei den Katholiken Bosniens und der Hercegovina. *Wissenschaftl. Mittheil. aus Bosnien und der Hercegovina* (Bosnisch-Hercegovinisches Landesmuseum in Sarajevo), VIENNA, 1896, v.4. Illustrated.

WUTTKE, H., Abbildungen zur Geschichte der Schrift. LEIPZIG, 1873.

Italian

ALBERTIS, O DE, Il tatuaggio delle prostitute; studio psicoanthropologica. GENOVA, 1888.

BERGÉ, Note sul tatuaggio nel manicomio guidiziario dell' Ambrogiana. *Cron. d.r. manicomio d'Ambrogiana,* FIRENZE, 1893.

BERTÉ, Il tatuaggio di Sicilia in rapporto alla resistenza psichica. *Arch. per. l'antropol.,* FIRENZE, 1892.

BLASIO, ABELE DE, Tatuaggi artistici in disertori francesi. *Archivio di antropologia criminale psichiatria e medicina legale,* TORINO, 1911, v.32.

CERCHOARI, G. LUIGI, Chiromanzio e tatuaggio. Note di varieta, ricerche storiche e scientifiche, coll' appendice di un' inchiesta con risposte di Ferrero, Mantegazza, Morselle ed altri. MILANO: V. Hoepeli, 1903 (bibliography appended).

CRECCIO, GUISEPPE DE, Studio sopra alcuni tatuaggi. *Archivio di psichiatria, neuropatologia, antropologia criminale,* TORINO, 1908, v.29 (ser. 3, v.5).

GIANI, P., Sopra un tatuaggio. *Archivio di antropologia criminale, psichiatria e medicina legale,* TORINO, 1910, v.31 (sec. 4, v.2). Illustrated.

GURRIERI, RAFFAELE, Il Tatuaggio nella Antropologia e nella Medicina Legale. BOLOGNA: N. Zanichelli, 1912.

LOMBROSO, CESARE, PROF., Sul tatuaggio degli Italiani. *Giornale di Medicina militare,* 1864.

Sul tatuaggio in Italia fra delinquenti. *Arch. per l'antropol.,* FIRENZE, 1874.

L'Uomo delinquente in rapporto all' antropologia, guirisprudenza e alle discipline carcerarie. TORINO, 1878 (contains a special chapter on tattooing).

Il tatuaggi nei criminali e nei pazzi secundo nuovi studi. *Arch. di psich.,* TORINO, 1893.

SANTANGELO, Tatuaggio, delinquenza; contributo all' anth. criminale. PISANI-PALERMO, 1891.

SEVERI, ALB., Il tatuaggio nei pazzi. *Arch. di psich.,* v. 6, p. 43.

Spanish

ALVAREZ, E., Tatuajes artisticos. *Plus ultra,* BUENOS AIRES, MARCH, 1920. Illustrated.

BACA, FRANCISCO MARTINEZ, DR., Los tatuages, estudio psicológico y médico-legal en delincuentes y militares. MEXICO: Oficina impresora del timbre, 1899. Illustrated.

index

index

index

index

index

index

index

A CATALOG OF SELECTED DOVER BOOKS IN ALL FIELDS OF INTEREST

100 BEST-LOVED POEMS, Edited by Philip Smith. "The Passionate Shepherd to His Love," "Shall I compare thee to a summer's day?" "Death, be not proud," "The Raven," "The Road Not Taken," plus works by Blake, Wordsworth, Byron, Shelley, Keats, many others. 96pp. 5³⁄₁₆ x 8¼. 0-486-28553-7

100 SMALL HOUSES OF THE THIRTIES, Brown-Blodgett Company. Exterior photographs and floor plans for 100 charming structures. Illustrations of models accompanied by descriptions of interiors, color schemes, closet space, and other amenities. 200 illustrations. 112pp. 8⅜ x 11. 0-486-44131-8

1000 TURN-OF-THE-CENTURY HOUSES: With Illustrations and Floor Plans, Herbert C. Chivers. Reproduced from a rare edition, this showcase of homes ranges from cottages and bungalows to sprawling mansions. Each house is meticulously illustrated and accompanied by complete floor plans. 256pp. 9⅜ x 12¼. 0-486-45596-3

101 GREAT AMERICAN POEMS, Edited by The American Poetry & Literacy Project. Rich treasury of verse from the 19th and 20th centuries includes works by Edgar Allan Poe, Robert Frost, Walt Whitman, Langston Hughes, Emily Dickinson, T. S. Eliot, other notables. 96pp. 5³⁄₁₆ x 8¼. 0-486-40158-8

101 GREAT SAMURAI PRINTS, Utagawa Kuniyoshi. Kuniyoshi was a master of the warrior woodblock print — and these 18th-century illustrations represent the pinnacle of his craft. Full-color portraits of renowned Japanese samurais pulse with movement, passion, and remarkably fine detail. 112pp. 8⅜ x 11. 0-486-46523-3

ABC OF BALLET, Janet Grosser. Clearly worded, abundantly illustrated little guide defines basic ballet-related terms: arabesque, battement, pas de chat, relevé, sissonne, many others. Pronunciation guide included. Excellent primer. 48pp. 4³⁄₁₆ x 5¾. 0-486-40871-X

ACCESSORIES OF DRESS: An Illustrated Encyclopedia, Katherine Lester and Bess Viola Oerke. Illustrations of hats, veils, wigs, cravats, shawls, shoes, gloves, and other accessories enhance an engaging commentary that reveals the humor and charm of the many-sided story of accessorized apparel. 644 figures and 59 plates. 608pp. 6 ⅛ x 9¼. 0-486-43378-1

ADVENTURES OF HUCKLEBERRY FINN, Mark Twain. Join Huck and Jim as their boyhood adventures along the Mississippi River lead them into a world of excitement, danger, and self-discovery. Humorous narrative, lyrical descriptions of the Mississippi valley, and memorable characters. 224pp. 5³⁄₁₆ x 8¼. 0-486-28061-6

ALICE STARMORE'S BOOK OF FAIR ISLE KNITTING, Alice Starmore. A noted designer from the region of Scotland's Fair Isle explores the history and techniques of this distinctive, stranded-color knitting style and provides copious illustrated instructions for 14 original knitwear designs. 208pp. 8⅜ x 10⅞. 0-486-47218-3

CATALOG OF DOVER BOOKS

ALICE'S ADVENTURES IN WONDERLAND, Lewis Carroll. Beloved classic about a little girl lost in a topsy-turvy land and her encounters with the White Rabbit, March Hare, Mad Hatter, Cheshire Cat, and other delightfully improbable characters. 42 illustrations by Sir John Tenniel. 96pp. 5³⁄₁₆ x 8¼. 0-486-27543-4

AMERICA'S LIGHTHOUSES: An Illustrated History, Francis Ross Holland. Profusely illustrated fact-filled survey of American lighthouses since 1716. Over 200 stations — East, Gulf, and West coasts, Great Lakes, Hawaii, Alaska, Puerto Rico, the Virgin Islands, and the Mississippi and St. Lawrence Rivers. 240pp. 8 x 10¾. 0-486-25576-X

AN ENCYCLOPEDIA OF THE VIOLIN, Alberto Bachmann. Translated by Frederick H. Martens. Introduction by Eugene Ysaye. First published in 1925, this renowned reference remains unsurpassed as a source of essential information, from construction and evolution to repertoire and technique. Includes a glossary and 73 illustrations. 496pp. 6⅛ x 9¼. 0-486-46618-3

ANIMALS: 1,419 Copyright-Free Illustrations of Mammals, Birds, Fish, Insects, etc., Selected by Jim Harter. Selected for its visual impact and ease of use, this outstanding collection of wood engravings presents over 1,000 species of animals in extremely lifelike poses. Includes mammals, birds, reptiles, amphibians, fish, insects, and other invertebrates. 284pp. 9 x 12. 0-486-23766-4

THE ANNALS, Tacitus. Translated by Alfred John Church and William Jackson Brodribb. This vital chronicle of Imperial Rome, written by the era's great historian, spans A.D. 14-68 and paints incisive psychological portraits of major figures, from Tiberius to Nero. 416pp. 5³⁄₁₆ x 8¼. 0-486-45236-0

ANTIGONE, Sophocles. Filled with passionate speeches and sensitive probing of moral and philosophical issues, this powerful and often-performed Greek drama reveals the grim fate that befalls the children of Oedipus. Footnotes. 64pp. 5³⁄₁₆ x 8 ¼. 0-486-27804-2

ART DECO DECORATIVE PATTERNS IN FULL COLOR, Christian Stoll. Reprinted from a rare 1910 portfolio, 160 sensuous and exotic images depict a breathtaking array of florals, geometrics, and abstracts — all elegant in their stark simplicity. 64pp. 8⅜ x 11. 0-486-44862-2

THE ARTHUR RACKHAM TREASURY: 86 Full-Color Illustrations, Arthur Rackham. Selected and Edited by Jeff A. Menges. A stunning treasury of 86 full-page plates span the famed English artist's career, from *Rip Van Winkle* (1905) to masterworks such as *Undine, A Midsummer Night's Dream,* and *Wind in the Willows* (1939). 96pp. 8⅜ x 11. 0-486-44685-9

THE AUTHENTIC GILBERT & SULLIVAN SONGBOOK, W. S. Gilbert and A. S. Sullivan. The most comprehensive collection available, this songbook includes selections from every one of Gilbert and Sullivan's light operas. Ninety-two numbers are presented uncut and unedited, and in their original keys. 410pp. 9 x 12. 0-486-23482-7

THE AWAKENING, Kate Chopin. First published in 1899, this controversial novel of a New Orleans wife's search for love outside a stifling marriage shocked readers. Today, it remains a first-rate narrative with superb characterization. New introductory Note. 128pp. 5³⁄₁₆ x 8¼. 0-486-27786-0

BASIC DRAWING, Louis Priscilla. Beginning with perspective, this commonsense manual progresses to the figure in movement, light and shade, anatomy, drapery, composition, trees and landscape, and outdoor sketching. Black-and-white illustrations throughout. 128pp. 8⅜ x 11. 0-486-45815-6

THE BATTLES THAT CHANGED HISTORY, Fletcher Pratt. Historian profiles 16 crucial conflicts, ancient to modern, that changed the course of Western civilization. Gripping accounts of battles led by Alexander the Great, Joan of Arc, Ulysses S. Grant, other commanders. 27 maps. 352pp. 5⅜ x 8½. 0-486-41129-X

BEETHOVEN'S LETTERS, Ludwig van Beethoven. Edited by Dr. A. C. Kalischer. Features 457 letters to fellow musicians, friends, greats, patrons, and literary men. Reveals musical thoughts, quirks of personality, insights, and daily events. Includes 15 plates. 410pp. 5⅜ x 8½. 0-486-22769-3

BERNICE BOBS HER HAIR AND OTHER STORIES, F. Scott Fitzgerald. This brilliant anthology includes 6 of Fitzgerald's most popular stories: "The Diamond as Big as the Ritz," the title tale, "The Offshore Pirate," "The Ice Palace," "The Jelly Bean," and "May Day." 176pp. 5⅜ x 8½. 0-486-47049-0

BESLER'S BOOK OF FLOWERS AND PLANTS: 73 Full-Color Plates from Hortus Eystettensis, 1613, Basilius Besler. Here is a selection of magnificent plates from the *Hortus Eystettensis,* which vividly illustrated and identified the plants, flowers, and trees that thrived in the legendary German garden at Eichstätt. 80pp. 8⅜ x 11. 0-486-46005-3

THE BOOK OF KELLS, Edited by Blanche Cirker. Painstakingly reproduced from a rare facsimile edition, this volume contains full-page decorations, portraits, illustrations, plus a sampling of textual leaves with exquisite calligraphy and ornamentation. 32 full-color illustrations. 32pp. 9⅜ x 12¼. 0-486-24345-1

THE BOOK OF THE CROSSBOW: With an Additional Section on Catapults and Other Siege Engines, Ralph Payne-Gallwey. Fascinating study traces history and use of crossbow as military and sporting weapon, from Middle Ages to modern times. Also covers related weapons: balistas, catapults, Turkish bows, more. Over 240 illustrations. 400pp. 7¼ x 10⅛. 0-486-28720-3

THE BUNGALOW BOOK: Floor Plans and Photos of 112 Houses, 1910, Henry L. Wilson. Here are 112 of the most popular and economic blueprints of the early 20th century — plus an illustration or photograph of each completed house. A wonderful time capsule that still offers a wealth of valuable insights. 160pp. 8⅜ x 11. 0-486-45104-6

THE CALL OF THE WILD, Jack London. A classic novel of adventure, drawn from London's own experiences as a Klondike adventurer, relating the story of a heroic dog caught in the brutal life of the Alaska Gold Rush. Note. 64pp. 5³⁄₁₆ x 8¼. 0-486-26472-6

CANDIDE, Voltaire. Edited by Francois-Marie Arouet. One of the world's great satires since its first publication in 1759. Witty, caustic skewering of romance, science, philosophy, religion, government — nearly all human ideals and institutions. 112pp. 5³⁄₁₆ x 8¼. 0-486-26689-3

CELEBRATED IN THEIR TIME: Photographic Portraits from the George Grantham Bain Collection, Edited by Amy Pastan. With an Introduction by Michael Carlebach. Remarkable portrait gallery features 112 rare images of Albert Einstein, Charlie Chaplin, the Wright Brothers, Henry Ford, and other luminaries from the worlds of politics, art, entertainment, and industry. 128pp. 8⅜ x 11. 0-486-46754-6

CHARIOTS FOR APOLLO: The NASA History of Manned Lunar Spacecraft to 1969, Courtney G. Brooks, James M. Grimwood, and Loyd S. Swenson, Jr. This illustrated history by a trio of experts is the definitive reference on the Apollo spacecraft and lunar modules. It traces the vehicles' design, development, and operation in space. More than 100 photographs and illustrations. 576pp. 6¾ x 9¼. 0-486-46756-2

A CHRISTMAS CAROL, Charles Dickens. This engrossing tale relates Ebenezer Scrooge's ghostly journeys through Christmases past, present, and future and his ultimate transformation from a harsh and grasping old miser to a charitable and compassionate human being. 80pp. 5 3/16 x 8 1/4. 0-486-26865-9

COMMON SENSE, Thomas Paine. First published in January of 1776, this highly influential landmark document clearly and persuasively argued for American separation from Great Britain and paved the way for the Declaration of Independence. 64pp. 5 3/16 x 8 1/4. 0-486-29602-4

THE COMPLETE SHORT STORIES OF OSCAR WILDE, Oscar Wilde. Complete texts of "The Happy Prince and Other Tales," "A House of Pomegranates," "Lord Arthur Savile's Crime and Other Stories," "Poems in Prose," and "The Portrait of Mr. W. H." 208pp. 5 3/16 x 8 1/4. 0-486-45216-6

COMPLETE SONNETS, William Shakespeare. Over 150 exquisite poems deal with love, friendship, the tyranny of time, beauty's evanescence, death, and other themes in language of remarkable power, precision, and beauty. Glossary of archaic terms. 80pp. 5 3/16 x 8 1/4. 0-486-26686-9

THE COUNT OF MONTE CRISTO: Abridged Edition, Alexandre Dumas. Falsely accused of treason, Edmond Dantès is imprisoned in the bleak Chateau d'If. After a hair-raising escape, he launches an elaborate plot to extract a bitter revenge against those who betrayed him. 448pp. 5 3/16 x 8 1/4. 0-486-45643-9

CRAFTSMAN BUNGALOWS: Designs from the Pacific Northwest, Yoho & Merritt. This reprint of a rare catalog, showcasing the charming simplicity and cozy style of Craftsman bungalows, is filled with photos of completed homes, plus floor plans and estimated costs. An indispensable resource for architects, historians, and illustrators. 112pp. 10 x 7. 0-486-46875-5

CRAFTSMAN BUNGALOWS: 59 Homes from "The Craftsman," Edited by Gustav Stickley. Best and most attractive designs from Arts and Crafts Movement publication — 1903–1916 — includes sketches, photographs of homes, floor plans, descriptive text. 128pp. 8 1/4 x 11. 0-486-25829-7

CRIME AND PUNISHMENT, Fyodor Dostoyevsky. Translated by Constance Garnett. Supreme masterpiece tells the story of Raskolnikov, a student tormented by his own thoughts after he murders an old woman. Overwhelmed by guilt and terror, he confesses and goes to prison. 480pp. 5 3/16 x 8 1/4. 0-486-41587-2

THE DECLARATION OF INDEPENDENCE AND OTHER GREAT DOCUMENTS OF AMERICAN HISTORY: 1775-1865, Edited by John Grafton. Thirteen compelling and influential documents: Henry's "Give Me Liberty or Give Me Death," Declaration of Independence, The Constitution, Washington's First Inaugural Address, The Monroe Doctrine, The Emancipation Proclamation, Gettysburg Address, more. 64pp. 5 3/16 x 8 1/4. 0-486-41124-9

THE DESERT AND THE SOWN: Travels in Palestine and Syria, Gertrude Bell. "The female Lawrence of Arabia," Gertrude Bell wrote captivating, perceptive accounts of her travels in the Middle East. This intriguing narrative, accompanied by 160 photos, traces her 1905 sojourn in Lebanon, Syria, and Palestine. 368pp. 5 3/8 x 8 1/2. 0-486-46876-3

A DOLL'S HOUSE, Henrik Ibsen. Ibsen's best-known play displays his genius for realistic prose drama. An expression of women's rights, the play climaxes when the central character, Nora, rejects a smothering marriage and life in "a doll's house." 80pp. 5 3/16 x 8 1/4. 0-486-27062-9

DOOMED SHIPS: Great Ocean Liner Disasters, William H. Miller, Jr. Nearly 200 photographs, many from private collections, highlight tales of some of the vessels whose pleasure cruises ended in catastrophe: the *Morro Castle, Normandie, Andrea Doria, Europa,* and many others. 128pp. 8⅞ x 11¾. 0-486-45366-9

THE DORÉ BIBLE ILLUSTRATIONS, Gustave Doré. Detailed plates from the Bible: the Creation scenes, Adam and Eve, horrifying visions of the Flood, the battle sequences with their monumental crowds, depictions of the life of Jesus, 241 plates in all. 241pp. 9 x 12. 0-486-23004-X

DRAWING DRAPERY FROM HEAD TO TOE, Cliff Young. Expert guidance on how to draw shirts, pants, skirts, gloves, hats, and coats on the human figure, including folds in relation to the body, pull and crush, action folds, creases, more. Over 200 drawings. 48pp. 8¼ x 11. 0-486-45591-2

DUBLINERS, James Joyce. A fine and accessible introduction to the work of one of the 20th century's most influential writers, this collection features 15 tales, including a masterpiece of the short-story genre, "The Dead." 160pp. 5³⁄₁₆ x 8¼. 0-486-26870-5

EASY-TO-MAKE POP-UPS, Joan Irvine. Illustrated by Barbara Reid. Dozens of wonderful ideas for three-dimensional paper fun — from holiday greeting cards with moving parts to a pop-up menagerie. Easy-to-follow, illustrated instructions for more than 30 projects. 299 black-and-white illustrations. 96pp. 8⅜ x 11. 0-486-44622-0

EASY-TO-MAKE STORYBOOK DOLLS: A "Novel" Approach to Cloth Dollmaking, Sherralyn St. Clair. Favorite fictional characters come alive in this unique beginner's dollmaking guide. Includes patterns for Pollyanna, Dorothy from *The Wonderful Wizard of Oz,* Mary of *The Secret Garden,* plus easy-to-follow instructions, 263 black-and-white illustrations, and an 8-page color insert. 112pp. 8¼ x 11. 0-486-47360-0

EINSTEIN'S ESSAYS IN SCIENCE, Albert Einstein. Speeches and essays in accessible, everyday language profile influential physicists such as Niels Bohr and Isaac Newton. They also explore areas of physics to which the author made major contributions. 128pp. 5 x 8. 0-486-47011-3

EL DORADO: Further Adventures of the Scarlet Pimpernel, Baroness Orczy. A popular sequel to *The Scarlet Pimpernel,* this suspenseful story recounts the Pimpernel's attempts to rescue the Dauphin from imprisonment during the French Revolution. An irresistible blend of intrigue, period detail, and vibrant characterizations. 352pp. 5³⁄₁₆ x 8¼. 0-486-44026-5

ELEGANT SMALL HOMES OF THE TWENTIES: 99 Designs from a Competition, Chicago Tribune. Nearly 100 designs for five- and six-room houses feature New England and Southern colonials, Normandy cottages, stately Italianate dwellings, and other fascinating snapshots of American domestic architecture of the 1920s. 112pp. 9 x 12. 0-486-46910-7

THE ELEMENTS OF STYLE: The Original Edition, William Strunk, Jr. This is the book that generations of writers have relied upon for timeless advice on grammar, diction, syntax, and other essentials. In concise terms, it identifies the principal requirements of proper style and common errors. 64pp. 5⅜ x 8½. 0-486-44798-7

THE ELUSIVE PIMPERNEL, Baroness Orczy. Robespierre's revolutionaries find their wicked schemes thwarted by the heroic Pimpernel — Sir Percival Blakeney. In this thrilling sequel, Chauvelin devises a plot to eliminate the Pimpernel and his wife. 272pp. 5³⁄₁₆ x 8¼. 0-486-45464-9

AN ENCYCLOPEDIA OF BATTLES: Accounts of Over 1,560 Battles from 1479 B.C. to the Present, David Eggenberger. Essential details of every major battle in recorded history from the first battle of Megiddo in 1479 B.C. to Grenada in 1984. List of battle maps. 99 illustrations. 544pp. 6½ x 9¼. 0-486-24913-1

ENCYCLOPEDIA OF EMBROIDERY STITCHES, INCLUDING CREWEL, Marion Nichols. Precise explanations and instructions, clearly illustrated, on how to work chain, back, cross, knotted, woven stitches, and many more — 178 in all, including Cable Outline, Whipped Satin, and Eyelet Buttonhole. Over 1400 illustrations. 219pp. 8⅜ x 11¼. 0-486-22929-7

ENTER JEEVES: 15 Early Stories, P. G. Wodehouse. Splendid collection contains first 8 stories featuring Bertie Wooster, the deliciously dim aristocrat and Jeeves, his brainy, imperturbable manservant. Also, the complete Reggie Pepper (Bertie's prototype) series. 288pp. 5⅜ x 8½. 0-486-29717-9

ERIC SLOANE'S AMERICA: Paintings in Oil, Michael Wigley. With a Foreword by Mimi Sloane. Eric Sloane's evocative oils of America's landscape and material culture shimmer with immense historical and nostalgic appeal. This original hardcover collection gathers nearly a hundred of his finest paintings, with subjects ranging from New England to the American Southwest. 128pp. 10⅝ x 9. 0-486-46525-X

ETHAN FROME, Edith Wharton. Classic story of wasted lives, set against a bleak New England background. Superbly delineated characters in a hauntingly grim tale of thwarted love. Considered by many to be Wharton's masterpiece. 96pp. 5³⁄₁₆ x 8 ¼. 0-486-26690-7

THE EVERLASTING MAN, G. K. Chesterton. Chesterton's view of Christianity — as a blend of philosophy and mythology, satisfying intellect and spirit — applies to his brilliant book, which appeals to readers' heads as well as their hearts. 288pp. 5⅜ x 8½. 0-486-46036-3

THE FIELD AND FOREST HANDY BOOK, Daniel Beard. Written by a co-founder of the Boy Scouts, this appealing guide offers illustrated instructions for building kites, birdhouses, boats, igloos, and other fun projects, plus numerous helpful tips for campers. 448pp. 5³⁄₁₆ x 8¼. 0-486-46191-2

FINDING YOUR WAY WITHOUT MAP OR COMPASS, Harold Gatty. Useful, instructive manual shows would-be explorers, hikers, bikers, scouts, sailors, and survivalists how to find their way outdoors by observing animals, weather patterns, shifting sands, and other elements of nature. 288pp. 5⅜ x 8½. 0-486-40613-X

FIRST FRENCH READER: A Beginner's Dual-Language Book, Edited and Translated by Stanley Appelbaum. This anthology introduces 50 legendary writers — Voltaire, Balzac, Baudelaire, Proust, more — through passages from *The Red and the Black, Les Misérables, Madame Bovary,* and other classics. Original French text plus English translation on facing pages. 240pp. 5⅜ x 8½. 0-486-46178-5

FIRST GERMAN READER: A Beginner's Dual-Language Book, Edited by Harry Steinhauer. Specially chosen for their power to evoke German life and culture, these short, simple readings include poems, stories, essays, and anecdotes by Goethe, Hesse, Heine, Schiller, and others. 224pp. 5⅜ x 8½. 0-486-46179-3

FIRST SPANISH READER: A Beginner's Dual-Language Book, Angel Flores. Delightful stories, other material based on works of Don Juan Manuel, Luis Taboada, Ricardo Palma, other noted writers. Complete faithful English translations on facing pages. Exercises. 176pp. 5⅜ x 8½. 0-486-25810-6

HEART OF DARKNESS, Joseph Conrad. Dark allegory of a journey up the Congo River and the narrator's encounter with the mysterious Mr. Kurtz. Masterly blend of adventure, character study, psychological penetration. For many, Conrad's finest, most enigmatic story. 80pp. 5$\frac{3}{16}$ x 8¼. 0-486-26464-5

HENSON AT THE NORTH POLE, Matthew A. Henson. This thrilling memoir by the heroic African-American who was Peary's companion through two decades of Arctic exploration recounts a tale of danger, courage, and determination. "Fascinating and exciting." — *Commonweal.* 128pp. 5⅜ x 8½. 0-486-45472-X

HISTORIC COSTUMES AND HOW TO MAKE THEM, Mary Fernald and E. Shenton. Practical, informative guidebook shows how to create everything from short tunics worn by Saxon men in the fifth century to a lady's bustle dress of the late 1800s. 81 illustrations. 176pp. 5⅜ x 8½. 0-486-44906-8

THE HOUND OF THE BASKERVILLES, Arthur Conan Doyle. A deadly curse in the form of a legendary ferocious beast continues to claim its victims from the Baskerville family until Holmes and Watson intervene. Often called the best detective story ever written. 128pp. 5$\frac{3}{16}$ x 8¼. 0-486-28214-7

THE HOUSE BEHIND THE CEDARS, Charles W. Chesnutt. Originally published in 1900, this groundbreaking novel by a distinguished African-American author recounts the drama of a brother and sister who "pass for white" during the dangerous days of Reconstruction. 208pp. 5⅜ x 8½. 0-486-46144-0

THE HUMAN FIGURE IN MOTION, Eadweard Muybridge. The 4,789 photographs in this definitive selection show the human figure — models almost all undraped — engaged in over 160 different types of action: running, climbing stairs, etc. 390pp. 7⅞ x 10⅝. 0-486-20204-6

THE IMPORTANCE OF BEING EARNEST, Oscar Wilde. Wilde's witty and buoyant comedy of manners, filled with some of literature's most famous epigrams, reprinted from an authoritative British edition. Considered Wilde's most perfect work. 64pp. 5$\frac{3}{16}$ x 8¼. 0-486-26478-5

THE INFERNO, Dante Alighieri. Translated and with notes by Henry Wadsworth Longfellow. The first stop on Dante's famous journey from Hell to Purgatory to Paradise, this 14th-century allegorical poem blends vivid and shocking imagery with graceful lyricism. Translated by the beloved 19th-century poet, Henry Wadsworth Longfellow. 256pp. 5$\frac{3}{16}$ x 8¼. 0-486-44288-8

JANE EYRE, Charlotte Brontë. Written in 1847, *Jane Eyre* tells the tale of an orphan girl's progress from the custody of cruel relatives to an oppressive boarding school and its culmination in a troubled career as a governess. 448pp. 5$\frac{3}{16}$ x 8¼. 0-486-42449-9

JAPANESE WOODBLOCK FLOWER PRINTS, Tanigami Kônan. Extraordinary collection of Japanese woodblock prints by a well-known artist features 120 plates in brilliant color. Realistic images from a rare edition include daffodils, tulips, and other familiar and unusual flowers. 128pp. 11 x 8¼. 0-486-46442-3

JEWELRY MAKING AND DESIGN, Augustus F. Rose and Antonio Cirino. Professional secrets of jewelry making are revealed in a thorough, practical guide. Over 200 illustrations. 306pp. 5⅜ x 8½. 0-486-21750-7

JULIUS CAESAR, William Shakespeare. Great tragedy based on Plutarch's account of the lives of Brutus, Julius Caesar and Mark Antony. Evil plotting, ringing oratory, high tragedy with Shakespeare's incomparable insight, dramatic power. Explanatory footnotes. 96pp. 5$\frac{3}{16}$ x 8¼. 0-486-26876-4

THE JUNGLE, Upton Sinclair. 1906 bestseller shockingly reveals intolerable labor practices and working conditions in the Chicago stockyards as it tells the grim story of a Slavic family that emigrates to America full of optimism but soon faces despair. 320pp. 5³⁄₁₆ x 8¼. 0-486-41923-1

THE KINGDOM OF GOD IS WITHIN YOU, Leo Tolstoy. The soul-searching book that inspired Gandhi to embrace the concept of passive resistance, Tolstoy's 1894 polemic clearly outlines a radical, well-reasoned revision of traditional Christian thinking. 352pp. 5³⁄₁₆ x 8¼. 0-486-45138-0

THE LADY OR THE TIGER?: and Other Logic Puzzles, Raymond M. Smullyan. Created by a renowned puzzle master, these whimsically themed challenges involve paradoxes about probability, time, and change; metapuzzles; and self-referentiality. Nineteen chapters advance in difficulty from relatively simple to highly complex. 1982 edition. 240pp. 5⅜ x 8½. 0-486-47027-X

LEAVES OF GRASS: The Original 1855 Edition, Walt Whitman. Whitman's immortal collection includes some of the greatest poems of modern times, including his masterpiece, "Song of Myself." Shattering standard conventions, it stands as an unabashed celebration of body and nature. 128pp. 5³⁄₁₆ x 8¼. 0-486-45676-5

LES MISÉRABLES, Victor Hugo. Translated by Charles E. Wilbour. Abridged by James K. Robinson. A convict's heroic struggle for justice and redemption plays out against a fiery backdrop of the Napoleonic wars. This edition features the excellent original translation and a sensitive abridgment. 304pp. 6⅛ x 9¼. 0-486-45789-3

LILITH: A Romance, George MacDonald. In this novel by the father of fantasy literature, a man travels through time to meet Adam and Eve and to explore humanity's fall from grace and ultimate redemption. 240pp. 5⅜ x 8½. 0-486-46818-6

THE LOST LANGUAGE OF SYMBOLISM, Harold Bayley. This remarkable book reveals the hidden meaning behind familiar images and words, from the origins of Santa Claus to the fleur-de-lys, drawing from mythology, folklore, religious texts, and fairy tales. 1,418 illustrations. 784pp. 5⅜ x 8½. 0-486-44787-1

MACBETH, William Shakespeare. A Scottish nobleman murders the king in order to succeed to the throne. Tortured by his conscience and fearful of discovery, he becomes tangled in a web of treachery and deceit that ultimately spells his doom. 96pp. 5³⁄₁₆ x 8¼. 0-486-27802-6

MAKING AUTHENTIC CRAFTSMAN FURNITURE: Instructions and Plans for 62 Projects, Gustav Stickley. Make authentic reproductions of handsome, functional, durable furniture: tables, chairs, wall cabinets, desks, a hall tree, and more. Construction plans with drawings, schematics, dimensions, and lumber specs reprinted from 1900s *The Craftsman* magazine. 128pp. 8⅛ x 11. 0-486-25000-8

MATHEMATICS FOR THE NONMATHEMATICIAN, Morris Kline. Erudite and entertaining overview follows development of mathematics from ancient Greeks to present. Topics include logic and mathematics, the fundamental concept, differential calculus, probability theory, much more. Exercises and problems. 641pp. 5⅜ x 8½. 0-486-24823-2

MEMOIRS OF AN ARABIAN PRINCESS FROM ZANZIBAR, Emily Ruete. This 19th-century autobiography offers a rare inside look at the society surrounding a sultan's palace. A real-life princess in exile recalls her vanished world of harems, slave trading, and court intrigues. 288pp. 5⅜ x 8½. 0-486-47121-7

THE METAMORPHOSIS AND OTHER STORIES, Franz Kafka. Excellent new English translations of title story (considered by many critics Kafka's most perfect work), plus "The Judgment," "In the Penal Colony," "A Country Doctor," and "A Report to an Academy." Note. 96pp. 5³⁄₁₆ x 8¼. 0-486-29030-1

MICROSCOPIC ART FORMS FROM THE PLANT WORLD, R. Anheisser. From undulating curves to complex geometrics, a world of fascinating images abound in this classic, illustrated survey of microscopic plants. Features 400 detailed illustrations of nature's minute but magnificent handiwork. The accompanying CD-ROM includes all of the images in the book. 128pp. 9 x 9. 0-486-46013-4

A MIDSUMMER NIGHT'S DREAM, William Shakespeare. Among the most popular of Shakespeare's comedies, this enchanting play humorously celebrates the vagaries of love as it focuses upon the intertwined romances of several pairs of lovers. Explanatory footnotes. 80pp. 5³⁄₁₆ x 8¼. 0-486-27067-X

THE MONEY CHANGERS, Upton Sinclair. Originally published in 1908, this cautionary novel from the author of *The Jungle* explores corruption within the American system as a group of power brokers joins forces for personal gain, triggering a crash on Wall Street. 192pp. 5⅜ x 8½. 0-486-46917-4

THE MOST POPULAR HOMES OF THE TWENTIES, William A. Radford. With a New Introduction by Daniel D. Reiff. Based on a rare 1925 catalog, this architectural showcase features floor plans, construction details, and photos of 26 homes, plus articles on entrances, porches, garages, and more. 250 illustrations, 21 color plates. 176pp. 8⅜ x 11. 0-486-47028-8

MY 66 YEARS IN THE BIG LEAGUES, Connie Mack. With a New Introduction by Rich Westcott. A Founding Father of modern baseball, Mack holds the record for most wins — and losses — by a major league manager. Enhanced by 70 photographs, his warmhearted autobiography is populated by many legends of the game. 288pp. 5⅜ x 8½. 0-486-47184-5

NARRATIVE OF THE LIFE OF FREDERICK DOUGLASS, Frederick Douglass. Douglass's graphic depictions of slavery, harrowing escape to freedom, and life as a newspaper editor, eloquent orator, and impassioned abolitionist. 96pp. 5³⁄₁₆ x 8¼. 0-486-28499-9

THE NIGHTLESS CITY: Geisha and Courtesan Life in Old Tokyo, J. E. de Becker. This unsurpassed study from 100 years ago ventured into Tokyo's red-light district to survey geisha and courtesan life and offer meticulous descriptions of training, dress, social hierarchy, and erotic practices. 49 black-and-white illustrations; 2 maps. 496pp. 5⅜ x 8½. 0-486-45563-7

THE ODYSSEY, Homer. Excellent prose translation of ancient epic recounts adventures of the homeward-bound Odysseus. Fantastic cast of gods, giants, cannibals, sirens, other supernatural creatures — true classic of Western literature. 256pp. 5³⁄₁₆ x 8¼. 0-486-40654-7

OEDIPUS REX, Sophocles. Landmark of Western drama concerns the catastrophe that ensues when King Oedipus discovers he has inadvertently killed his father and married his mother. Masterly construction, dramatic irony. Explanatory footnotes. 64pp. 5³⁄₁₆ x 8¼. 0-486-26877-2

ONCE UPON A TIME: The Way America Was, Eric Sloane. Nostalgic text and drawings brim with gentle philosophies and descriptions of how we used to live — self-sufficiently — on the land, in homes, and among the things built by hand. 44 line illustrations. 64pp. 8⅜ x 11. 0-486-44411-2

ONE OF OURS, Willa Cather. The Pulitzer Prize–winning novel about a young Nebraskan looking for something to believe in. Alienated from his parents, rejected by his wife, he finds his destiny on the bloody battlefields of World War I. 352pp. $5\frac{3}{16}$ x $8\frac{1}{4}$. 0-486-45599-8

ORIGAMI YOU CAN USE: 27 Practical Projects, Rick Beech. Origami models can be more than decorative, and this unique volume shows how! The 27 practical projects include a CD case, frame, napkin ring, and dish. Easy instructions feature 400 two-color illustrations. 96pp. $8\frac{1}{4}$ x 11. 0-486-47057-1

OTHELLO, William Shakespeare. Towering tragedy tells the story of a Moorish general who earns the enmity of his ensign Iago when he passes him over for a promotion. Masterly portrait of an archvillain. Explanatory footnotes. 112pp. $5\frac{3}{16}$ x $8\frac{1}{4}$. 0-486-29097-2

PARADISE LOST, John Milton. Notes by John A. Himes. First published in 1667, *Paradise Lost* ranks among the greatest of English literature's epic poems. It's a sublime retelling of Adam and Eve's fall from grace and expulsion from Eden. Notes by John A. Himes. 480pp. $5\frac{3}{16}$ x $8\frac{1}{4}$. 0-486-44287-X

PASSING, Nella Larsen. Married to a successful physician and prominently ensconced in society, Irene Redfield leads a charmed existence — until a chance encounter with a childhood friend who has been "passing for white." 112pp. $5\frac{3}{8}$ x $8\frac{1}{2}$. 0-486-43713-2

PERSPECTIVE DRAWING FOR BEGINNERS, Len A. Doust. Doust carefully explains the roles of lines, boxes, and circles, and shows how visualizing shapes and forms can be used in accurate depictions of perspective. One of the most concise introductions available. 33 illustrations. 64pp. $5\frac{3}{8}$ x $8\frac{1}{2}$. 0-486-45149-6

PERSPECTIVE MADE EASY, Ernest R. Norling. Perspective is easy; yet, surprisingly few artists know the simple rules that make it so. Remedy that situation with this simple, step-by-step book, the first devoted entirely to the topic. 256 illustrations. 224pp. $5\frac{3}{8}$ x $8\frac{1}{2}$. 0-486-40473-0

THE PICTURE OF DORIAN GRAY, Oscar Wilde. Celebrated novel involves a handsome young Londoner who sinks into a life of depravity. His body retains perfect youth and vigor while his recent portrait reflects the ravages of his crime and sensuality. 176pp. $5\frac{3}{16}$ x $8\frac{1}{4}$. 0-486-27807-7

PRIDE AND PREJUDICE, Jane Austen. One of the most universally loved and admired English novels, an effervescent tale of rural romance transformed by Jane Austen's art into a witty, shrewdly observed satire of English country life. 272pp. $5\frac{3}{16}$ x $8\frac{1}{4}$. 0-486-28473-5

THE PRINCE, Niccolò Machiavelli. Classic, Renaissance-era guide to acquiring and maintaining political power. Today, nearly 500 years after it was written, this calculating prescription for autocratic rule continues to be much read and studied. 80pp. $5\frac{3}{16}$ x $8\frac{1}{4}$. 0-486-27274-5

QUICK SKETCHING, Carl Cheek. A perfect introduction to the technique of "quick sketching." Drawing upon an artist's immediate emotional responses, this is an extremely effective means of capturing the essential form and features of a subject. More than 100 black-and-white illustrations throughout. 48pp. 11 x $8\frac{1}{4}$. 0-486-46608-6

RANCH LIFE AND THE HUNTING TRAIL, Theodore Roosevelt. Illustrated by Frederic Remington. Beautifully illustrated by Remington, Roosevelt's celebration of the Old West recounts his adventures in the Dakota Badlands of the 1880s, from roundups to Indian encounters to hunting bighorn sheep. 208pp. $6\frac{1}{4}$ x $9\frac{1}{4}$. 0-486-47340-6

THE RED BADGE OF COURAGE, Stephen Crane. Amid the nightmarish chaos of a Civil War battle, a young soldier discovers courage, humility, and, perhaps, wisdom. Uncanny re-creation of actual combat. Enduring landmark of American fiction. 112pp. 5³⁄₁₆ x 8¼. 0-486-26465-3

RELATIVITY SIMPLY EXPLAINED, Martin Gardner. One of the subject's clearest, most entertaining introductions offers lucid explanations of special and general theories of relativity, gravity, and spacetime, models of the universe, and more. 100 illustrations. 224pp. 5⅜ x 8½. 0-486-29315-7

REMBRANDT DRAWINGS: 116 Masterpieces in Original Color, Rembrandt van Rijn. This deluxe hardcover edition features drawings from throughout the Dutch master's prolific career. Informative captions accompany these beautifully reproduced landscapes, biblical vignettes, figure studies, animal sketches, and portraits. 128pp. 8⅜ x 11. 0-486-46149-1

THE ROAD NOT TAKEN AND OTHER POEMS, Robert Frost. A treasury of Frost's most expressive verse. In addition to the title poem: "An Old Man's Winter Night," "In the Home Stretch," "Meeting and Passing," "Putting in the Seed," many more. All complete and unabridged. 64pp. 5³⁄₁₆ x 8¼. 0-486-27550-7

ROMEO AND JULIET, William Shakespeare. Tragic tale of star-crossed lovers, feuding families and timeless passion contains some of Shakespeare's most beautiful and lyrical love poetry. Complete, unabridged text with explanatory footnotes. 96pp. 5³⁄₁₆ x 8¼. 0-486-27557-4

SANDITON AND THE WATSONS: Austen's Unfinished Novels, Jane Austen. Two tantalizing incomplete stories revisit Austen's customary milieu of courtship and venture into new territory, amid guests at a seaside resort. Both are worth reading for pleasure and study. 112pp. 5⅜ x 8½. 0-486-45793-1

THE SCARLET LETTER, Nathaniel Hawthorne. With stark power and emotional depth, Hawthorne's masterpiece explores sin, guilt, and redemption in a story of adultery in the early days of the Massachusetts Colony. 192pp. 5³⁄₁₆ x 8¼. 0-486-28048-9

THE SEASONS OF AMERICA PAST, Eric Sloane. Seventy-five illustrations depict cider mills and presses, sleds, pumps, stump-pulling equipment, plows, and other elements of America's rural heritage. A section of old recipes and household hints adds additional color. 160pp. 8⅜ x 11. 0-486-44220-9

SELECTED CANTERBURY TALES, Geoffrey Chaucer. Delightful collection includes the General Prologue plus three of the most popular tales: "The Knight's Tale," "The Miller's Prologue and Tale," and "The Wife of Bath's Prologue and Tale." In modern English. 144pp. 5³⁄₁₆ x 8¼. 0-486-28241-4

SELECTED POEMS, Emily Dickinson. Over 100 best-known, best-loved poems by one of America's foremost poets, reprinted from authoritative early editions. No comparable edition at this price. Index of first lines. 64pp. 5³⁄₁₆ x 8¼. 0-486-26466-1

SIDDHARTHA, Hermann Hesse. Classic novel that has inspired generations of seekers. Blending Eastern mysticism and psychoanalysis, Hesse presents a strikingly original view of man and culture and the arduous process of self-discovery, reconciliation, harmony, and peace. 112pp. 5³⁄₁₆ x 8¼. 0-486-40653-9

SKETCHING OUTDOORS, Leonard Richmond. This guide offers beginners step-by-step demonstrations of how to depict clouds, trees, buildings, and other outdoor sights. Explanations of a variety of techniques include shading and constructional drawing. 48pp. 11 x 8¼. 0-486-46922-0

SMALL HOUSES OF THE FORTIES: With Illustrations and Floor Plans, Harold E. Group. 56 floor plans and elevations of houses that originally cost less than $15,000 to build. Recommended by financial institutions of the era, they range from Colonials to Cape Cods. 144pp. 8⅜ x 11. 0-486-45598-X

SOME CHINESE GHOSTS, Lafcadio Hearn. Rooted in ancient Chinese legends, these richly atmospheric supernatural tales are recounted by an expert in Oriental lore. Their originality, power, and literary charm will captivate readers of all ages. 96pp. 5⅜ x 8½. 0-486-46306-0

SONGS FOR THE OPEN ROAD: Poems of Travel and Adventure, Edited by The American Poetry & Literacy Project. More than 80 poems by 50 American and British masters celebrate real and metaphorical journeys. Poems by Whitman, Byron, Millay, Sandburg, Langston Hughes, Emily Dickinson, Robert Frost, Shelley, Tennyson, Yeats, many others. Note. 80pp. 5³⁄₁₆ x 8¼. 0-486-40646-6

SPOON RIVER ANTHOLOGY, Edgar Lee Masters. An American poetry classic, in which former citizens of a mythical midwestern town speak touchingly from the grave of the thwarted hopes and dreams of their lives. 144pp. 5³⁄₁₆ x 8¼. 0-486-27275-3

STAR LORE: Myths, Legends, and Facts, William Tyler Olcott. Captivating retellings of the origins and histories of ancient star groups include Pegasus, Ursa Major, Pleiades, signs of the zodiac, and other constellations. "Classic." — *Sky & Telescope.* 58 illustrations. 544pp. 5⅜ x 8½. 0-486-43581-4

THE STRANGE CASE OF DR. JEKYLL AND MR. HYDE, Robert Louis Stevenson. This intriguing novel, both fantasy thriller and moral allegory, depicts the struggle of two opposing personalities — one essentially good, the other evil — for the soul of one man. 64pp. 5³⁄₁₆ x 8¼. 0-486-26688-5

SURVIVAL HANDBOOK: The Official U.S. Army Guide, Department of the Army. This special edition of the Army field manual is geared toward civilians. An essential companion for campers and all lovers of the outdoors, it constitutes the most authoritative wilderness guide. 288pp. 5³⁄₁₆ x 8¼. 0-486-46184-X

A TALE OF TWO CITIES, Charles Dickens. Against the backdrop of the French Revolution, Dickens unfolds his masterpiece of drama, adventure, and romance about a man falsely accused of treason. Excitement and derring-do in the shadow of the guillotine. 304pp. 5³⁄₁₆ x 8¼. 0-486-40651-2

TEN PLAYS, Anton Chekhov. *The Sea Gull, Uncle Vanya, The Three Sisters, The Cherry Orchard,* and *Ivanov,* plus 5 one-act comedies: *The Anniversary, An Unwilling Martyr, The Wedding, The Bear,* and *The Proposal.* 336pp. 5³⁄₁₆ x 8¼. 0-486-46560-8

THE FLYING INN, G. K. Chesterton. Hilarious romp in which pub owner Humphrey Hump and friend take to the road in a donkey cart filled with rum and cheese, inveighing against Prohibition and other "oppressive forms of modernity." 320pp. 5⅜ x 8½. 0-486-41910-X

THIRTY YEARS THAT SHOOK PHYSICS: The Story of Quantum Theory, George Gamow. Lucid, accessible introduction to the influential theory of energy and matter features careful explanations of Dirac's anti-particles, Bohr's model of the atom, and much more. Numerous drawings. 1966 edition. 240pp. 5⅜ x 8½. 0-486-24895-X

TREASURE ISLAND, Robert Louis Stevenson. Classic adventure story of a perilous sea journey, a mutiny led by the infamous Long John Silver, and a lethal scramble for buried treasure — seen through the eyes of cabin boy Jim Hawkins. 160pp. 5³⁄₁₆ x 8¼. 0-486-27559-0

THE TRIAL, Franz Kafka. Translated by David Wyllie. From its gripping first sentence onward, this novel exemplifies the term "Kafkaesque." Its darkly humorous narrative recounts a bank clerk's entrapment in a bureaucratic maze, based on an undisclosed charge. 176pp. 5³⁄₁₆ x 8¼. 0-486-47061-X

THE TURN OF THE SCREW, Henry James. Gripping ghost story by great novelist depicts the sinister transformation of 2 innocent children into flagrant liars and hypocrites. An elegantly told tale of unspoken horror and psychological terror. 96pp. 5³⁄₁₆ x 8¼. 0-486-26684-2

UP FROM SLAVERY, Booker T. Washington. Washington (1856-1915) rose to become the most influential spokesman for African-Americans of his day. In this eloquently written book, he describes events in a remarkable life that began in bondage and culminated in worldwide recognition. 160pp. 5³⁄₁₆ x 8¼. 0-486-28738-6

VICTORIAN HOUSE DESIGNS IN AUTHENTIC FULL COLOR: 75 Plates from the "Scientific American – Architects and Builders Edition," 1885-1894, Edited by Blanche Cirker. Exquisitely detailed, exceptionally handsome designs for an enormous variety of attractive city dwellings, spacious suburban and country homes, charming "cottages" and other structures — all accompanied by perspective views and floor plans. 80pp. 9¼ x 12¼. 0-486-29438-2

VILLETTE, Charlotte Brontë. Acclaimed by Virginia Woolf as "Brontë's finest novel," this moving psychological study features a remarkably modern heroine who abandons her native England for a new life as a schoolteacher in Belgium. 480pp. 5³⁄₁₆ x 8¼. 0-486-45557-2

THE VOYAGE OUT, Virginia Woolf. A moving depiction of the thrills and confusion of youth, Woolf's acclaimed first novel traces a shipboard journey to South America for a captivating exploration of a woman's growing self-awareness. 288pp. 5³⁄₁₆ x 8¼. 0-486-45005-8

WALDEN; OR, LIFE IN THE WOODS, Henry David Thoreau. Accounts of Thoreau's daily life on the shores of Walden Pond outside Concord, Massachusetts, are interwoven with musings on the virtues of self-reliance and individual freedom, on society, government, and other topics. 224pp. 5³⁄₁₆ x 8¼. 0-486-28495-6

WILD PILGRIMAGE: A Novel in Woodcuts, Lynd Ward. Through startling engravings shaded in black and red, Ward wordlessly tells the story of a man trapped in an industrial world, struggling between the grim reality around him and the fantasies his imagination creates. 112pp. 6⅛ x 9¼. 0-486-46583-7

WILLY POGÁNY REDISCOVERED, Willy Pogány. Selected and Edited by Jeff A. Menges. More than 100 color and black-and-white Art Nouveau–style illustrations from fairy tales and adventure stories include scenes from Wagner's "Ring" cycle, *The Rime of the Ancient Mariner, Gulliver's Travels,* and *Faust.* 144pp. 8⅜ x 11. 0-486-47046-6

WOOLLY THOUGHTS: Unlock Your Creative Genius with Modular Knitting, Pat Ashforth and Steve Plummer. Here's the revolutionary way to knit — easy, fun, and foolproof! Beginners and experienced knitters need only master a single stitch to create their own designs with patchwork squares. More than 100 illustrations. 128pp. 6½ x 9¼. 0-486-46084-3

WUTHERING HEIGHTS, Emily Brontë. Somber tale of consuming passions and vengeance — played out amid the lonely English moors — recounts the turbulent and tempestuous love story of Cathy and Heathcliff. Poignant and compelling. 256pp. 5³⁄₁₆ x 8¼. 0-486-29256-8